Contents

To the memory of Eliza Anna
and John William Miles,
whose parental guidance
kept Johnny on the right road,
and to Katherine Williston.

Author's Notes

From the balcony of his highrise apartment on Hamilton Mountain, Johnny Miles has a panoramic view of the city he adopted in 1927. In the distance, he can see Ivor Wynne Stadium, formerly known as Hamilton Civic Stadium. After his family followed him from Cape Breton, Nova Scotia, to Hamilton and purchased a house on Balsam Avenue—across the street from the stadium—his father would lean out of the house's third-floor window and time Johnny as he ran laps in the stadium at night. Later, Johnny sat on the stoop of the house with Olympic sprint champion Percy Williams and other members of the Canadian track and field team who participated in the first British Empire Games, held in Hamilton in 1930. In his mind, Johnny can follow the route he ran in the marathon event, winning a bronze medal. As he recounted the story of that win during a visit in October 1986, I could almost hear the cheers of 17,000 spectators echoing in the bleachers.

Looking at the city from another angle, Johnny can see the buildings and gate of the former International Harvester plant. Johnny spent 20 years in that plant before giving the company another 23 years of service in Europe and in the United States. Today, the Harvester sign is gone, but its outline is clearly visible.

Inside the apartment is an array of personal items that Johnny and his wife, Bess, have acquired during more than 50 years together. There are the two gold medals that Johnny won at the Boston marathons of 1926 and 1929, mementos from two Olympiads, and countless other trophies and awards. In his study, Johnny sits and reflects on his many lives: English immigrant, boy miner in Cape Breton, teamster, Sunday-school teacher, local hero, "Marathon King," international executive, member of the

Order of Canada and of the Nova Scotia and Canadian sports halls of fame, and patron of an annual marathon that bears his name.

During the course of that 1986 visit, the Mileses received a telephone call and then a visit from Roland Lepers, an old friend who was in Canada on business. Lepers had been one of the first Frenchmen the couple encountered after International Harvester transferred them to France in 1947. He told me that while living in France for seven years, Johnny had barely mentioned his days of running and breaking records.

I was not surprised. Johnny is a modest man who talked openly of the love and respect he feels for his late parents and for his family, who were so instrumental in his early days of running. He spoke warmly of the many runners against whom he had competed in the 1920s and 1930s and was concerned that I understand the era in which he rose from the grim conditions of a Cape Breton coal-mining town to international athletic stardom. But most of all, as he tapped his memory and opened up the old scrapbooks for the writing of this book, Johnny urged that I be forthright in assessing his career, warts and all.

Ten years earlier, I had first discussed the possibility of writing a book about Johnny's life with Bruce Kidd, a former Canadian Press athlete of the year who was guest speaker at the first running of the annual Johnny Miles Marathon in New Glasgow, Nova Scotia. It could serve, we concluded in New Glasgow, as both a piece of history and as an example to today's emerging athletes. Kidd returned to Toronto and I to Winnipeg, but it was not until my attention was drawn to the book *Canada's Sporting Heroes* and the piece on Johnny and other runners of his era that I began in earnest this labor of love.

Many people have had input during this rather protracted process, some contributing greatly and others providing bits of information that led me eventually to other sources. I want to thank them first. Despite the inexplicable headline that I stared at in the April 20, 1926, edition of the *Manitoba Free Press*—"NOVA SCOTIA YOUTH WINS 305TH BOSTON A.A. MARATHON"—that newspaper and library, the Winnipeg Centennial Public Library, served as rich resources during much of my research. However, without a doubt, it was Johnny's scrapbooks—mostly the work of his father and of his brother, Tom—that provided the most extensive collection of clippings and photographs. I want to thank Johnny and Bess for their patience in answering many questions via letters and in subsequent interviews. Their kindness in opening up their home and their hearts to me greatly eased my research tasks.

I was fortunate that Dr. John Miles Williston, founder of the annual

Miles marathon, is family. Instead of becoming agitated with my continuous demands, he and the Miles Marathon Committee responded graciously to all of my requests and provided encouragement at the most appropriate times. Originally, I planned to end the book with the inauguration of the Miles marathon, but as it grew in size and stature, the marathon became a more essential piece of Johnny's post-retirement period. In this regard, a special thanks is owing to the staff of the *New Glasgow Evening News* for their extensive coverage of the Miles marathon and for the many photographs they made available. Thanks, as well, to the *Pictou Advocate* and to my many other newspaper sources.

My appreciation to the following individuals: Ed O'Toole, Andy MacDonald, Gina MacDonald, Gerald MacDonald, Charlie Pye, Jimmie Hawboldt, Will Cloney, Roy Oliver, Duncan Taylor, E.D. MacNaughton, Malcolm Williston, the late Sam Keeling, the late Peter Campbell, Neil MacMullin, the relatives of Silas McLellan, C.M. Mosher, Hamilton mayor R.M. Morrow, Barbara Marsh, and Yud MacKinnon. If I have missed anyone, may my thanks be with you.

A debt of gratitude is due to these sources: Cheryl Rielly, Canadian Sports Hall of Fame; Tom Sweet, Nova Scotia Sports Heritage Hall of Fame; Frank W. Graham, Newfoundland Sports Archives; Joseph Hansen, Novistar Corporation; Theresa Haley, alumni records, St. Francis Xavier University; Robert Johnson, Lally archivist, Tufts University.

In addition to the Winnipeg Centennial and the Henderson Highway public libraries, much thanks to University of Manitoba Dafoe Library, Halifax City Regional Library, Public Archives of Nova Scotia, Boston Public Library, records of the Boston Marathon, St. Francis Xavier University, Hamilton Public Library, McMaster University Extension Library, and Cape Breton Regional Library.

I am indeed indebted to Bruce Kidd, Dr. Sandy Young, Fergie MacKay, Shirley and George Manos, and Johnny and Phyllis Williston for taking the time from their busy schedules to read and critique the manuscript.

Thanks to Judy in Winnipeg, for her work and patience in typing the first two drafts, and to Elsie, for her patience and understanding. A special thanks to John K. Lynn, the key to bringing together the manuscript, the publisher, Dorothy Blythe, and the editor, Susan LeBlanc. It is my hope that their confidence in this project—not only for the benefit of sports history but for the Johnny Mileses of tomorrow—will be justified.

Floyd Williston

Preface

Athletes have always inspired the Canadian imagination. We are drawn to their energy, their grace and playfulness, their ambition and daring. When they win, we rejoice and walk tall and tackle the problems of our own lives with renewed confidence. When they lose or are disgraced, we weep openly with them and agonize over their sins and shortcomings, as if they were our children or our closest friends. And, in a way, they are, for they are usually nurtured by whole communities, not only with the material help of funds and facilities but also with the accumulated lore of generations and with the hopes and open affection of neighbors and complete strangers alike.

But except for professional hockey players, Canadians are often ignorant of our best athletes, especially those of another region or generation. Sports-trivia buffs can rattle off the starting line-ups of Major League Baseball or National Basketball Association teams but cannot name a single member of the men's or women's teams that represent Canada in Olympic and other international competitions. Thanks to Canadian novelist W.P. Kinsella, many of us are familiar with the tragedy of "Shoeless Joe" Jackson, an American who was expelled from baseball after the gambling scandal of 1919; but how many know about the exploits of early Canadian baseball stars such as James "Tip" O'Neill, from Woodstock, Ontario, who batted .435 in the majors in 1887 and was the best hitter of his time?

It was much the same when I was growing up in the 1950s. I wanted to run in the Olympics, but I had no Canadian role models. The only track stars I knew about were British or American.

There is a reason for this. Throughout the century, the Canadian sports media—the main source of our ideas about sport—have been dominated by corporate interests increasingly dependent upon and attracted to the American market. Well before the Canadian Press wire service was established in the 1920s, Canadian newspapers relied on Associated Press for their out-of-town news. Not surprisingly, the result was a heavy diet of American sports news. A study of sports coverage in Halifax, Montreal, Toronto, Winnipeg, and Vancouver in the 1920s and 1930s found that 15 of the 20 most-frequently mentioned athletes were American. (The sole Canadian was boxer Jimmy McLarnin.)

The same pattern can be seen on television, even on the publicly owned CBC. In the summer, Major League Baseball, with two franchises and seven farm teams in Canada, dominates the airwaves. The featured American and Caribbean athletes are gifted and exciting to watch, but it is difficult for young Canadians to identify with them because they come from somewhere else. It reinforces the idea that it is not possible to come from Canada and excel.

In these circumstances, Floyd Williston's readable biography of marathoner Johnny Miles is doubly welcome. It is not only an insightful account of the career of one of Canada's best athletes, it also recaptures the character and accomplishments of an important earlier period in Canadian sport, the years between the two world wars.

In the age before lavish prizes, appearance fees, and endorsement contracts for long-distance running, athletes trained long and hard, prepared race plans with care and cunning, and fiercely competed for the love of the sport and the challenge of the contest. Miles and many of his competitors grew up and trained under extremely trying economic and social conditions. They had none of the specialized equipment and medical support athletes take for granted today. Yet they achieved marvellous feats, gave great pleasure to those who saw them race, and brought pride to their friends and communities.

Miles' life is a powerful lesson in the value of persistent determination and systematic reflection. Despite early hardships, he kept at it with a buoyant optimism, carefully drawing lessons from his early defeats, surprising everyone but himself and his father-coach to defeat Olympic champion Albin Stenroos, of Finland, to win the 1926 Boston Marathon. When he failed to win the following year, sceptics were quick to write him off, but he bounced back to win it again in 1929 and enjoy a distinguished career in the Olympic and British Empire games. After his running days were over, he applied the same qualities to his work and became a successful business executive. He is still an honored contributor to Canadian road racing.

Miles' life also shows that individuals can overcome some of the inequalities of class and region. Growing up in the remote coal town of Sydney Mines, Cape Breton, where harsh labor practices kept mining families to bare subsistence, Miles started out with none of the advantages of big-city athletes. But, in addition to his own considerable abilities, he had one priceless asset: the support of his family and community. Later, he found the same community support in another labor town, Hamilton, Ontario.

There is much to be learned from this book—about Miles and his competitors, the many contributions Nova Scotia and Hamilton have made to Canadian sport, and the way social conditions shape the nature of opportunities. Williston has gone far beyond the headlines in both his research and his analysis.

My only regret is that the book was not available when I was a young runner, so I could have trained in the confidence that other Canadians had competed internationally with success. We should be able to choose our heroes from the men and the women who have lived and excelled in our midst. Johnny Miles is certainly one of them.

Bruce Kidd

Introduction

In 1926, I was already an avid sports follower. Even to a 14-year-old, no single event was more interesting, more exciting, than the annual Boston Athletic Association Marathon.

More than half a century later, the situation is the same. With the exception of the National Football League's Super Bowl, the marathon attracts the largest crowds, achieves the greatest worldwide attention of any other one-day sports event.

I watched the 1926 race from Beacon Street, about two miles from the finish line on Exeter Street, in front of the stately BAA clubhouse. My vantage point was relatively uncrowded, the view of the runners clear, in contrast to the mob scene at the finish, where perhaps 10,000 spectators turned the narrow area into something resembling Times Square on New Year's Eve.

Like everyone else, I anticipated a spirited duel between local hero Clarence DeMar—eventually a seven-time winner—and Olympic marathon champion Albin Stenroos, of Finland. And, like everybody else, I was amazed to see a chunky, determined unknown, a dark horse in the truest sense, ahead of the field in the last stretch of one of the greatest victories in marathon history, in Boston or anywhere else.

The unknown did not remain anonymous for long. By the time he crossed the finish line, he had been identified as John C. Miles, a grocery-cart driver from Sydney Mines, Nova Scotia. Most Bostonians would have a hard time locating Nova Scotia on the map; to locate Sydney Mines took more ingenuity. John was as quiet and reserved as any 20-year-old would be among the stars of marathoning. As his story unfolded, it took on the dimensions of a fairy tale, embellished as it was by the print media. In those days before television, the Boston and suburban papers, the national and international press, had a field day, as the story was much more appealing than a victory by DeMar or Stenroos would have been.

As a sports fan who knew about the marathon from the time he could read, as a sportswriter who covered the race from 1930 to 1956, and as the director of the race from 1946 to 1982, I have a valid long-term perspective. From that viewpoint, I can say without equivocation: There will never be another Johnny Miles. My reasoning is sound. Johnny was a complete unknown in Boston in 1926. Without fanfare, he was entered in the race along with dozens of others from Canada and the United States. Unlike DeMar and Stenroos, his fame had not preceded him, because, quite truthfully, he had not achieved much fame, even in the faraway stretches of Canada. And in all the years since then, no one without some marathoning experience has won the famous race. While great runners from around the world followed him through the years, there has been no surprise ending to match 1926 and the grocery-cart driver from Nova Scotia. When Johnny won the marathon again in 1929, it came as no surprise.

How things have changed in the intervening years. A sport that was purely amateur has become crassly commercial, a hybrid that threatens to destroy itself. Marathoning has grown from a few races a year into an enterprise that offers a major race a week, to say nothing of shorter distances—and even longer ones—that crowd the calendar. The physical demands of a marathon are such that few runners should compete in more than two or three a year. But every four years, the situation is exacerbated because two of these three races will be the Olympic trials and then the Olympics.

Race directors have become race promoters. The success of their production rests with sponsorship, and sponsorship depends on the number of well-known runners in your race. The circle is indeed vicious.

Thankfully, there are exceptions to the rule. One is the annual Johnny Miles Marathon in New Glasgow, Nova Scotia, motivated by the desire to keep the memory of Johnny's feats firmly planted in the history of Canadian athletics. Yesterday's hero can be soon forgotten, but nobody will forget Johnny if these people, the dozens of public-spirited men and women in that warm and friendly community, have anything to say about it.

They have reason to be proud, not only of his athletic accomplishments but also of his exemplary lifestyle of more than eight decades.

Johnny does not know it, but on many occasions when I have been asked to speak to large groups, I have used his life as an example of what can be accomplished through dedication and motivation.

The springboard to Johnny's success in life came through athletics. The two Boston victories opened doors that would normally remain shut for an obscure youngster from a tiny town. Once those doors opened, however, Johnny could not trade on his gold medals. He had to produce, to prove himself, to answer the challenge. He did so without losing any of his humility, without trampling on the rights of others, without sustaining anything but a positive attitude towards life. These are the marks of a true sportsman.

These are the marks of Johnny Miles.

Will Cloney

"The marathon is the acme of athletic heroism."
—Roger Bannister

"To be a runner, you have to run a marathon. To be a marathoner, you have to run the Boston."
—unidentified California runner

1 The First Crowning

As the snow began to melt and the winds blowing off the Atlantic changed to cool breezes, Johnny Miles and his father decided the time was ripe to attempt a full marathon.

Johnny had never seen a full-length marathon—let alone run one. But at age 20, the Cape Bretoner held the Canadian five-mile foot-racing title and the Maritime 10-mile championship. In the fall of 1925, he had set a record in the Herald and Mail 10-Mile Modified Marathon, a popular event. He carried in his pocket a crumpled picture of Albin Stenroos, Finnish winner of the marathon at the 1924 Paris Olympics, and he dreamed of running the Boston Marathon. He had been running for only a few years.

A light snow blanketed Cape Breton on Good Friday, 1926, as Johnny rode the train to a point approximately 27 miles outside of Sydney Mines. He got off and began running home through the snow, slush, and mud. When he greeted his father two hours and 40 minutes later, Mr. Miles was ecstatic. "Son," he said, "I think you're ready for Boston."

Johnny had a feeling that he could do even better in Boston, particularly if there was no snow on the ground.

Leading up to the Patriot's Day race—which traditionally, but not always, fell on April 19—Johnny's mother paid special attention to her son's diet, sometimes depriving herself. She checked that he was sleeping well and kept him well supplied with clean running gear.

Meanwhile, the family worried about its finances for the trip. Johnny had saved some of the money he made delivering groceries for the local co-operative store, and his parents—who planned to root Johnny on in Boston—had limited funds. But supporters in the coal-mining region had begun collecting money for the runner, who was already something of a celebrity. And despite the grim economic situation, organizers were able to present Johnny with a purse containing $300—about three months' wages for a grocery-cart driver.

In Boston, expatriate Cape Bretoners were rallying behind the young hopeful. Peter Campbell, formerly of Johnstown, Cape Breton, had read an article in a Nova Scotia newspaper describing Johnny's intention to tackle the famed race. Unknown to Johnny, Campbell wrote to the elder Miles with an offer to arrange things on that end. Mr. Miles accepted immediately and wrote that the family would need accommodation in a private home or boarding house, as Mrs. Miles wanted to cook for her son. The Lynch family, distant relatives of the Campbells, agreed to put the Mileses up in their Jamaica Plain home. Murdock Campbell, formerly of Inverness County, offered to drive Johnny and his father along the marathon route before race day and to chauffeur them to the race, and the Davidsons, formerly of Sydney Mines, invited the family to dinner in their Boston home.

Interaction among eastern-Canadian and New England athletes was common. It was usually more convenient for someone like Johnny to travel to neighboring areas of the United States than it was to compete in Ontario or Quebec.

On departure day, about 50 people gathered at the Sydney Mines railway station to see the family off. On board, passengers approached the dark-haired, ruddy-cheeked runner to shake his hand and wish him luck. "You're sure to get a place, John," said one well-meaning fellow, "but I hardly expect you to win over the great stars who will be there." Undeterred, Johnny responded calmly, "I'm not going to get a place—I'm going to Boston to win."

Arriving a few days early so he could familiarize himself with the city, Johnny was immediately impressed with the size of Boston and with the fast pace. "Everyone seemed to be going somewhere," he recalls. "I was anxious about finding somewhere to stay. I didn't know that my father had already made the arrangements."

Leaving Mrs. Miles at the Lynches' house, Johnny and his father called at the offices of the Boston Athletic Association to pick up information on the race, and a map. To the officials present that day, Johnny was just another unknown, and race manager Tom Kanaly was amused when the kid admitted to never having run a race longer than 10 miles. With a few comments about Stenroos and local runner Clarence DeMar being in top form, Kanaly wished Johnny a cold "good luck." Feeling slighted, Johnny turned and shot back a few parting words. "Don't be disappointed if I win the race on the 19th," he said. "Perhaps you've already picked the man to win this race, but I'm telling you now that I'm going to win the race."

The press was not paying Johnny much heed, either. Other Canadians—including Silas McLellan, of Hants County, Nova Scotia; Arthur Scholes and Charles Snell, of Toronto—topped the list of non-Americans being given an outside chance of beating Stenroos and DeMar, a frequent winner.

On April 18, the day before the race, Murdock Campbell drove Johnny and his father-coach along the marathon course, pointing out strategic streets along the way. The names imprint themselves on the mind of anyone who has ever entered the classic: South Frampton, Nanton, Wellesley Square, Lower Newton, Lake Street, and the notorious Newton hills, the bane of more than one potential winner. At Hopkinton, the starting point of the race, Johnny and his father climbed out of the car and told their driver that they would walk the 26 or so miles back to Boston. They wanted to examine every landmark, obstacle, twist, and turn.

They did not figure on getting lost. Stopping a policeman to ask for directions, they explained that they had just arrived and were following the race route so Johnny would not get lost later. "Don't worry, sir," the policeman said with a smile, "just let your son follow the crowd. Just follow the crowd, and he'll find his way all right."

The usually restrained Mr. Miles piped up, "My son is going to lead the crowd, and so it is necessary that he know the right way."

"Let's hope so," said the policeman, pointing out where they had turned right when they should have turned left.

Back at the Lynches' house, Mrs. Miles was preparing supper, plus a steak that Johnny had requested for a cold pre-race lunch. As it grew dark and her husband and son did not return, she grew worried. Tomorrow, Johnny would face the greatest challenge of his young life.

It was well after dark before Johnny and his dad sat down to supper. Afterwards, Mr. Miles gave his son a vigorous rubdown, discussed their final strategy, and left Johnny to get a good night's sleep. But as his parents fielded telephone calls and visits from well-wishers, Johnny tossed in his bed. He spent an unusually restless night, as he realized the magnitude of the goal he had set for himself.

The Boston newspapers the next morning sang the praises of Stenroos and DeMar. One or two sportswriters acknowledged Johnny's presence in the city, calling him "untrained" and a "raw youth." Johnny was quoted as saying that if he lost, that simply meant that a better runner had won. He mentioned the debt he owed his parents and said that he wanted to win for them and for Cape Breton.

About 9 a.m., Murdock Campbell arrived to drive Johnny to the race starting point at the Tebeau farm, in Hopkinton. During the half-hour journey, Campbell said little. He was probably worried about Johnny's chances.

Few people shared Johnny's confidence. His recent victories were considered insignificant, because he had not run a marathon; and it was thought that no one as young as he could possibly do better than the cream of the marathon world. But the runner possessed a quiet self-assurance, born in the Cape Breton coal mines where he had gone to work at age 11 and fortified by the support of his family and community.

Johnny and his father also believed in their simple strategy: stick to the heels of the front runners and make a last-minute sprint to the finish. The tactic had proven effective in other, shorter races.

In the cramped farmhouse that served for weigh-ins and was some-times called the Ashland clubhouse, Johnny mingled with the other runners. When Whitey Michelson overheard Johnny suggesting that he had as good a chance at winning as anyone else, the marathon world-record holder broke into the conversation. "What's that you say, you ... win? What's your name?" Michelson asked.

"Jack Miles," Johnny replied.

"You have a fine chance to win today," Michelson said sarcastically.

"Well, you just watch me. I'll be in the shower before the second-place runner comes in. You wait and see," Johnny countered, not knowing to whom he was speaking.

"You're crazy," Michelson shot back. "You're another one of those marathon nuts they talk about."

"All right," Johnny said. "Just wait and see."

Michelson's doubts were probably shared by the bystanders who stared as Johnny sat on the sidewalk, eating cold steak and dry toast and washing it down with tea. He did not look like a serious challenger, and he was certainly not acting like one. More than one passer-by also remarked on Johnny's sneakers, which he had purchased at the co-operative store in Sydney Mines for 98 cents.

The noon starting time was approaching, and Johnny was excited. At five feet six-and-a-half inches and 133 pounds, he was declared fit to run. He remembers feeling "on top of the world." "Number 14" wore a white jersey featuring a red maple leaf and the superimposed letters "NS."

As the field of 96 runners gathered at the starting line, Johnny managed to position himself next to the two runners he respected the most—Stenroos and DeMar. With his father giving him last-minute advice, Johnny received a big good-luck kiss and a fresh handkerchief from his mother, who said, stepping to the sidelines, "See you at the finish line."

Everyone present was taken aback to see a middle-aged woman at the starting line of a race then entered solely by men. "Hey, kid, do you expect to win?" came a wisecracking voice from the midst of the runners.

"Well, Pa says I can run a bit," Johnny offered.

Thinking about his father's final instructions to "stay with the leaders and do your best for Nova Scotia and Cape Breton," Johnny recalled the scene at the Sydney Mines railway station. Mayor Mike Dwyer had shaken Johnny's hand and advised solemnly, "Johnny, when you get to Boston, you'll be up against many seasoned runners, and no doubt you'll become very tired during the long race. But always remember the man next to you may be just as tired. So, no matter how tired you feel, remember that you can always make one more step, and that may be the one to carry you across the finish line."

The gun sounded, and the pack of runners lurched forward. Johnny was in front, slightly behind Stenroos and DeMar, and his mind was on the finish line, 26 miles, 385 yards away. His father's voice kept ringing in his ears: "Stay with Stenroos, stay with DeMar."

At the seven-mile mark, Stenroos increased his pace unexpectedly, leaving the others wondering about his strategy. Johnny decided to stay with DeMar, mindful that DeMar held the course record and that he probably had his own plan. Soon after, he realized nervously that Stenroos was now out of sight. Faithful to his father's advice, Johnny passed DeMar with a short burst of speed, but he was shocked to see that two other runners were already between him and Stenroos. "I passed Michelson and Number 81, whoever that was, and came within a short distance of the front runner, Stenroos," Johnny recalls.

He continued in that position for some time, intentionally not pressing Stenroos until he noticed, at the 22-mile marker at Newton hills, that the Olympic champion was slowing down. Johnny was now in full stride. Earlier, a sharp pain in his side had worried him briefly, but it had gradually subsided, and from that point onward, Johnny ran in his unique high-stepping style.

With four miles remaining to the finish line, Johnny had to be decisive. He put on a burst of speed and came shoulder to shoulder with the leader. Hesitating to pass, Johnny glanced over at Stenroos and saw a strange look on the leader's face. His eyes seemed sunken and glassy. "I decided that now was the time to make my move," he says. "I never looked back, fearing that I might provoke him into a duel. When I went past him at Lake Street, I knew then that I would win. He had that old stitch that has killed off so many runners. When I saw him rubbing his side, I hit my pace a little bit stronger. That was enough to take the heart out of him."

When the finish line came into view, Johnny had enough energy left for one more sprint. To the amazement of everyone there except his parents, the unknown from Sydney Mines hit the tape at 2:25.40.4—a new course record and a world record.

Newspaper reporters rushed to interview the new champion, who did not even appear winded. This "darkest of dark horses" had proven everyone wrong, but he was more concerned with finding his parents than with discussing his performance. He withheld comment on the race, wanting to hear his father's assessment of it, but he did suggest that he could probably run back to Hopkinton without too much effort.

He made his way to the clubhouse, and as he had promised Michelson, he was under the shower before the second runner crossed the finish line. Stenroos needed four more minutes to reach the finish; DeMar was third. As for Michelson, who finished fourth, he would not forget the name of the winner. He and Johnny would clash several times over the next few years; they would also become good friends.

Outside the door of the clubhouse, Mr. Miles was having a hard time convincing a policeman that he was the father and trainer of the new champion. When he was finally allowed in, Mr. Miles rushed right into the shower and gave his son a bear hug. With the locker-room crowd looking on in amazement, Johnny and his father stood under the shower like two silly schoolboys. The pant legs and coat sleeves of Mr. Miles' new suit shrank a couple of inches under the soaking.

Asked 60 years later to describe his feelings on breaking the tape, Johnny was as excited as he likely was on April 19, 1926. "It is difficult to describe the feeling of joy at that moment. After many months of planning and training, and sacrifice by my parents, the pressure was now off and the mission accomplished," he says. "I was rushed into the clubhouse before I could see my mother and thank her. I was very moved by the words of praise from Stenroos and DeMar. I felt very proud and pleased to shake hands with two of the world's greatest athletes. It was the beginning of a lifelong friendship, especially with DeMar, with whom I have shared many a starting line before my racing career came to an end."

Stenroos and DeMar raved about the upstart, the first Canadian to win the Boston Marathon in 11 years. "He's a wonderful runner," DeMar told a reporter. "If, at his age, he can better my record by four minutes, I don't know what he'll do when he's my age." Stenroos said he was "beaten by a better runner. Miles is one of the best I've ever seen."

BAA officials called Johnny "the best marathoner to ever win here."

As the Boston press scurried for background material on this unknown, one enterprising reporter overheard Johnny asking where he could send a telegram to his girl in Sydney Mines. The reporter rushed over to the Lynches' house and asked Peter Campbell to open Johnny's suitcase, in case there was a picture there that the paper could publish. Campbell remembers being so upset that he told the reporter to leave instantly. Johnny has never revealed the recipient of the "Finished First" telegram.

As soon as word reached Sydney Mines, preparations were under way for the biggest reception the town had ever arranged. It was said that for several days, all conversation in Cape Breton centred around Johnny.

At the Miles home, brother Tom and sisters Lena and Lillian enjoyed their own celebration. When he learned from the Sydney Mines telegraph office that his brother had won, Tom, along with a friend, tried to raise a flag on the front lawn. But in the process, the flagpole fell across the streetcar tracks, and just then a trolley car came along. When the driver heard that Johnny had come first in Boston, he got off the streetcar and helped the boys raise the flag while the passengers cheered.

After finishing his shower, Johnny hardly had time to get dressed before the telegrams and other messages began pouring in. But the most important greeting was the one he received from his mother as he left the clubhouse. He was not the least bit embarrassed as she took him in her arms and planted a kiss on his cheek. If it had not been for Johnny, she never would have visited Boston. Now she felt as if the whole city were hers.

That evening and the next day, the papers broke the news. It was not long before they were proclaiming Johnny "Marathon King." The *Boston Post* splashed a headline across the front page, "UNKNOWN KID SMASHES RECORD IN GREATEST OF ALL MARATHONS." "BOSTON GOES WILD OVER JOHN C. MILES, C.B. SUPERMAN," bragged the Sydney, Nova Scotia, *Record*. The *Boston Traveller* called Johnny's win "one of the biggest surprise victories ever." "Confidence in self, as distinguished from conceit, and this confidence bred of deep respect for parental advice, plus a keen and alert brain, makes John C. Miles of Sydney Mines, Cape Breton, Canada, an international figure today," the *Traveller's* Frank Ryan wrote. "A lad of 20 years, smartened by wise words of a world-wise father, rather than from the teachings of books, slow of tongue but quick of thought, he stands today a marked marathon runner, conqueror of the Olympic Champion, Albin Stenroos of Finland, and the greatest of American runners, Clarence DeMar of Melrose." Suggesting that Johnny was the stuff of fiction, Ryan compared Johnny's life to that of the Merriwell boys, in the popular children's books written by Burt Standish.

Johnny recalls that among the milling crowd after the race were two Nova Scotians who took a great interest in him: J.E. "Gee" Ahern, a former sports editor for the Halifax *Herald* who was then working in the area; and Victor MacAulay, from Windsor, Nova Scotia, a frequent entrant in the Boston Marathon. Ahern, who would become one of Johnny's strongest supporters, wrote of the race: "John C. Miles, the plucky Cape Breton boy, in winning today's American marathon completely changed the world's athletic history.... He is tonight, technically, the champion long distance runner in the world."

Johnny and his parents had intended to return to Sydney Mines the day after the race but stayed in Boston for another week. They received more than 50 invitations from churches, service associations, radio stations, and sports clubs, and the *Boston Post* treated them to a two-day tour of the city. Perley Barbour, the mayor of the suburb of Quincy, even bought Johnny a new suit.

The *Post* tour—led by state troopers and met everywhere by hundreds of people—included luncheons, visits to schools and places of work, speeches in city squares, and civic receptions at several Boston suburban town halls. Johnny visited Charlestown Prison, was escorted to a boxing match, and played umpire as the first pitch was thrown to open the National Baseball League season. For two days, his itinerary was printed on the newspaper's front page.

Receptions, dances, and banquets followed at the Hotel Somerset, hosted by the Canadian Club; in Roxbury, thanks to the Cape Breton Club; and at the Lenox Hotel, where expatriate Cape Bretoners honored the hero. Johnny had no trouble regaining the four pounds he had shed during the marathon.

On Monday, April 26, Johnny and his parents finally boarded a train for home. The delivery boy from Cape Breton had become the toast of

Boston, offered advice to school children, signed autographs, and given countless speeches. Through it all, the clean-living, modest runner must have seemed a breath of fresh air. Here was a young man who really meant it when he said, "Everything I am today, I owe to my parents."

Enjoying the relative calm of the train, the Mileses could hardly imagine the reception they would receive upon crossing into Canada. They had read in the Boston papers about the numerous post-victory celebrations throughout Nova Scotia, of the blowing of whistles at the coal mines and the steel plant, of the unfurling of flags, and of the outpouring of praise. But they did not expect to be received in a fashion usually reserved for royalty.

Johnny and his mother (right), at the Sydney Mines railway station.

Boston Marathon, 1926.

Victory tour after Boston Marathon, 1926. Johnny (centre) is flanked by his parents.

Johnny receives the winner's gold medal.

Receives a new suit in Boston.

Interviewed on radio.

2 A New Life

Johnny first entered Canada in 1906. Early that year, four-month-old John Christopher, his mother, Eliza, and two-year-old sister Lena steamed into Saint John, New Brunswick, where John Miles, Sr., waited at the dock. They boarded a train for Cape Breton, and during the journey, Mr. Miles acquainted himself with the son he had never met.

Although Mr. Miles had written frequently over the past few months of his new life in the coal-mining town of Florence, his wife was not prepared for the rows of company houses and the unpaved streets. Exhausted after her long journey from Halifax, Yorkshire, England, Mrs. Miles hardly reacted when her husband stopped in front of one of the row houses on Pitt Street and announced, "Children, we're home at last."

Mr. Miles, a former streetcar operator from Cardiff, Wales, had been lured to Canada's east coast in 1905 by the booming coal and steel industry. On Cape Breton Island, company towns sprang up around the pitheads in Glace Bay, North Sydney, Dominion, Sydney Mines, and Florence; and representatives of the two major coal companies in the region—Dominion Coal, and Nova Scotia Steel and Coal—headed for Europe to recruit workers. They painted a rosy picture of high wages and pleasant living conditions on the pretty island. Thousands of men accepted the offer of free passage to Canada.

In Wales, England, and Scotland, militant strikes had created considerable hardship for miners and their families. The Canadian recruiters had not mentioned that unrest was also prevalent among Nova Scotia miners, who were forming workers' associations in a fight for better working conditions and higher pay.

Mr. Miles soon found himself mining coal in the No. 1 Princess Mine, miles below the Atlantic Ocean. The work was back-breaking and the wages low, but he stuck with it, dreaming of the day when he could afford to send for his pregnant wife and little daughter.

Mrs. Miles overcame her initial disappointment and soon had the house in tiptop shape, stretching her husband's wages in order to feed and clothe her family. There were few luxuries, but the family was able to avoid sinking too far into debt with the company stores.

In every mining community in Nova Scotia, particularly where the company was the only major employer, the companies controlled almost all retail trade. Clothing, footwear, groceries, crockery, furniture, and even linoleum could be purchased in the two-storey wooden shops. To tempt youngsters like Johnny and his friends, the store displayed, in colorful array, glass jars of chocolates, jelly beans, lollipops, peanut brittle, and fudge. Behind the stores—all constructed alike—a shed held bales of hay and feed that could be had for horses, cattle, and other livestock. The quality of the goods, from butter to bullets, was generally excellent, and the near-monopoly position meant that inventory was usually fresh and plentiful.

Shopping was no problem: Credit was extended to all coal-company employees. Weekly purchases were deducted from a miner's wages, along with his rent, coal, light, water, medical, church, and blasting-powder charges—all neatly recorded on a "bobtailed sheet." The miners' pay sheets were so dubbed because of the system of cutting off the bottom to show that the employee had no wages coming to him. In winter, when mining operations were cut back or suspended because coal ships could not sail out of Cape Breton, debts mounted. Miners in debt had no choice but to continue working for the company in order to pay off their tabs at the "pluck-me stores."

This dependence became a powerful management tool when workers complained about cutbacks or demanded better working conditions. All credit was cut off, or threats were made to this end, and woes were sometimes compounded by eviction from the company house.

The opening of the first co-operative store in Florence was seen as something of a godsend. A branch of the British Canadian Co-operative Society in Sydney Mines, the Florence structure had previously belonged to one of the coal companies. But customers to this store were co-op members, and they had a say in its operation.

The Miles family joined the co-op, as well as the local credit union and the Presbyterian-United Church. Joined by Tom, born in 1908, and Lillian, born seven years later, they participated in co-op activities such as annual picnics, a town band, choir, theatrical group, and literary society.

Eager to move beyond the exhausting, dangerous work at the coal face, Mr. Miles attended night school and took a correspondence course. By 1913, he had earned a mine manager's certificate.

Three years later, Mr. Miles, a veteran of the Boer War, decided to join the Canadian Army and do his part in the world war that had been raging since 1914. After a short period of basic training, he was shipped overseas to France as part of the Nova Scotia Highlanders.

With the departure of the family breadwinner, 11-year-old Johnny offered to quit school and work in the mine. His parents owed money on a new house they had built on Green Hill; and such was the benevolence of mine management that it allowed child labor for the sake of the war effort. Johnny's mother flatly refused to let her son leave school, so he suggested he continue his studies but work an afternoon shift after school. Mrs. Miles gave in.

Tom recalls that mine officials first rejected Johnny because he was too small. "The next time he applied, he wore mother's high-heel shoes so that he could see over the employment manager's desk, and [he] was hired to clean the miners' lamps." Mr. Miles consented to the arrangement, allowing the company to hire Johnny at 35 cents an hour, from 3 p.m. to 11 p.m. six days a week, in the No. 4 mine, Florence. Soon, Johnny was bringing home a pay envelope every Saturday. It always contained 15 to 18 dollars, less deductions.

Not surprisingly, Johnny's schoolwork suffered because of his job. But the sleep he so dearly needed eluded him as images of rats, water dripping from the ocean above, and rumbling coal trains filled his thoughts. The situation worsened when Johnny was transferred underground and made a "trapper."

Only those who have worked in a mine can appreciate what a demanding, dirty, dangerous job it was. Johnny was already 12 years old when he started to work the trapdoors and share the shift with children who were even younger. Alone in the awful darkness, with the hiss of escaping gas and the creaking of roof props the only sounds, Johnny's task was to control the ventilation doors that allowed pony-led loads of coal to pass through—and kept dangerous gases from accumulating at the mine face.

One of his workmates was Sam Selfridge, who recalled those days in a 1989 letter to Johnny: "When we worked together, Jackie, you were driving a horse named Dell ... I was driving Kelly. You and I used to 'wrastle' when we were waiting for empty cars. After you left I got a score-horse and was paid 10 cents a ton. The first man I saw killed was Herb Watson ... he had gone through WWI without a scratch. Another, Jackie Odoux, was killed of a broken neck and ribs through his lungs...."

Another story about those children who toiled in the mines is told by Gordon MacGregor, a former superintendent of mines in Nova Scotia. He recounts how one of his cousins, who was younger than Johnny, was obliged to work in the pit because of his father's death. A small, timid boy, he was forced to walk through a graveyard on his way to work. Although he was brave enough to work in the dark, rat-infested mine, he would not travel alone through the cemetery. So his mother rose with him, in the darkness of the early morning, and took her son by the hand to work.

Johnny had no aversion to rats. At mealtime, he often fed them a soiled corner of his sandwich, and their very presence was a good sign, meaning that no gas was leaking. His greatest fear was that something would happen to his father overseas. Meanwhile, Mrs. Miles worried that something would happen to her son.

The family was fortunate: Mr. Miles returned with only a superficial shrapnel wound, and Johnny escaped coal mining without major injury.

It was an excited 13-year-old who met the troop train that carried his father home in 1919. Johnny and his father had always been close, and no one had absorbed the letters from overseas more keenly than the boy forced to leave his childhood behind. His eyes light up as he recalls that day:

> My father returned with only minor wounds. He and Uncle Oscar, a sergeant major, fought at Vimy Ridge, in France, where so many Canadians made the supreme sacrifice. I remember how we would rush to the train station every time a troop train stopped in Florence before going on to North Sydney and Sydney. Many trains went by, and we would return home disappointed that my dad wasn't on one of them. Eventually, some time after Uncle Oscar had returned, we received a telegram informing us that Dad would be arriving on the next train. I became very excited and decided to walk along the tracks to Little Bras d'Or and meet the train at an earlier station. When the train stopped there for some soldiers to disembark, I sneaked aboard and let it be known that I was looking for my father, Sergeant John Miles. Word spread around, and I finally located him before arriving at the next station. It was a happy

occasion for both of us. His knapsack and kit-bags were bulging at the seams, and I remember how anxious I was to get home and see what the bags contained. The rest of the family was waiting at the Florence station. After this happy, but tearful, reunion with my father, we all walked from the station to our house. My father was anxious to take up his life again where he'd left off nearly four years before.

After a period of rest and spending time with his family, Mr. Miles returned to the pit as overman, underground. He soon realized that he had not missed the mine work at all and set his sights on other work.

Johnny quit the mine, concentrated on his studies, and chummed around with his close friends Billy MacDonald and Davey Robinson. When he entered high school, he had an opportunity to play rugby, as his father had done. And at his father's urging, Johnny began training as a boxer. Mr. Miles, winner of an amateur boxing title in England, encouraged the training as part of an overall fitness program.

In the loft of the barn, behind the Miles house on Green Hill, Johnny could be frequently seen doing push-ups, lifting weights, and pounding at the punching bag. A regular visitor was Sam Keeling, a local short-distance runner. Keeling could not see much promise in Johnny as a boxer but encouraged him to take up road racing. One day, he dropped off a book on running written by well-known British runner Alf Shrubb.

3 A 98-Pound Bag of Flour

Johnny's entry into the world of competitive running was not so noble as one might imagine. It was not the cheer of the crowd or the thrill of seeing his picture in the newspaper that attracted the 16-year-old high-school student but the possibility of winning some otherwise unobtainable prizes. This he could not resist.

On various occasions, he had seen handwritten posters in the window of the British Canadian Co-operative Store that advertised road races in Sydney, North Sydney, and Sydney Mines. He knew a few of the local boys who ran, and once or twice watched Sam Keeling in short-distance races. But when he saw the assortment of prizes being offered to the winners of the 1922 three-mile Victoria Day race in Sydney, he was hooked.

The sponsor of the race, Sydney merchant Nate Nathansan, had set up a display in a sporting-goods-store window. Johnny stared at the tempting array of items on display, which would be awarded to the first 16 finishers in the May 24 race. At that moment, Johnny made up his mind to get in shape and try middle-distance running.

"Imagine," he thought, "how wonderful it would be to win a fishing rod and reel or an all-purpose jack-knife." These were things other boys could expect to own, but to Johnny, they were luxuries. "We just couldn't afford them," Johnny explains years later.

On returning home, Johnny's first act was to dig out the Shrubb book that Sam Keeling had given him. Then he went outside, in his regular street clothes, and sprinted down the road to see how far he could get without becoming winded. Although expecting the worst, he surprised himself.

His lungs were in better shape than one might expect considering his exposure to dust and dampness in the mines.

Encouraged by this test, he began to follow the instructions in the Shrubb manual, word for word. When he became winded, he walked a while and then ran another 50 yards, walking and running until he had completed a mile. During a four-week period, he increased his pace to a mile and a half, upping it to two miles, and then completing three miles without running out of breath. Training in the cool of the evening and in the early morning, Johnny shared his dreams with only one person, Keeling.

Keeling could not believe his eyes the first time he saw Johnny running along the roadside, and he admonished him to slow down before he exhausted himself. Although he sometimes found the pace too strenuous for his short, skinny legs, Keeling began running along with his ambitious friend. He figured Johnny had what it took to become a good runner. "Gee, Jack, you're a born runner," he said.

To attend the Victoria Day race in Sydney, Johnny and his friend Archie MacLean travelled by bus, ferry, streetcar, and on foot. Johnny wore a pair of trousers cut off just above the knee, a white undershirt, and a pair of low, flat-soled sneakers. Race officials were dismayed when he asked to enter the main event—the three-mile race for the Nathansan cup—and someone suggested that he enter the junior events. When advised that he would be running against 75 competitors and some of the best middle-distance runners in Nova Scotia, Johnny shrugged his shoulders.

Somewhat intimidated by the 3,000 to 4,000 spectators and by the confident, seasoned runners, Johnny said a silent prayer as he took his place at the starting line. At the signal, he was off with the rest of the pack but soon dropped back. He finished 17th but rationalized that at least he had not been last. Reid Ross, of Sydney, won the race in 17:3.

"So I didn't win a prize," Johnny reflected on the way home, "but just wait till next time."

Johnny's father was not happy with the effort. Johnny and MacLean found Mr. Miles in the garden, and he stopped his work long enough to listen to Johnny's enthusiastic report of the race. Then he asked if Johnny planned to enter more races, and Johnny replied, "Of course. Remember the advice you're always giving to others: if at first you don't succeed ..." But by this time, Mr. Miles was engrossed in his gardening.

Luckily, Johnny was undeterred.

The poster advertising the 1922 Dominion Day race in North Sydney listed, among other goodies, a 98-pound bag of Robin Hood flour that a nearby merchant was offering to the first runner to pass his shop. Johnny mailed in an entry form for the three-mile event and devised a strategy.

As the runners gathered at the starting line on race day, Johnny edged towards the front. When the gun sounded, he bolted and never looked back. Only the thought of bringing that bag of flour home to his mother kept him from collapsing. He maintained his pace, passing the shop before anyone else and placing third overall.

Johnny came home not only with the sack of flour but also with a small wooden table lamp that was the third-place prize. His mother was pleased, and his father's interest was tweaked. He said that "perhaps" he would attend his son's next race.

The training was beginning to pay off, but Johnny knew that he had to expand on his limited strategy. Running too fast, too soon, could take its toll. Several times, Johnny caught a glimpse of his father looking out of the window as Johnny ran past the house, wearing basketball shorts and dirty sneakers.

A month later, Mr. Miles took the entire family to a three-mile race in Sydney Mines. Johnny's fourth-place finish elicited this response from his father: "You just may have the potential to be a fair runner. I'll teach you the finer things about the sport, so you can be a great runner."

Thus began a coach-athlete relationship that would take Johnny to the summit of marathoning. Mr. Miles was dedicated to his family and to his new job as manager of the Jubilee Colliery—which moved the family to Sydney Mines in 1923—but he made a decision to devote all of his spare time to Johnny's fledgling running career. He had recognized in "son Jack" a natural ability.

In Johnny's opinion, his father could do no wrong. A good listener, he nevertheless held firm views. He taught by example, always conscious of the role model he was providing his children and neighbors. An elder in the Presbyterian-United Church, he did not drink and rarely smoked. Johnny recalls many occasions when his father encouraged him and his siblings to undertake such tasks as negotiating the purchase of a wagon. But when it came to matters of training and race strategy, Mr. Miles was boss.

Before long, the open space behind the Mileses' Greener's Point home was transformed into a makeshift, eighth-of-a-mile track, with "Coach Miles" handling the stopwatch as Johnny ran laps. Shrubb's manual became a "second bible" in the household—and Johnny's passport to Boston.

In the fall of 1922, Johnny entered Grade 11 for what would be his last year of school. He had a reputation as a strong swimmer, and when he donned a pair of skates, he became the envy of his schoolmates. Wearing a pair of speed skates, he could frequently be seen gliding along the wind-cleared surface of Little Pond. But nothing could replace what was quickly becoming Johnny's first love—road racing.

During the next two years, Johnny would enter every major middle-distance road race in the province. He concentrated on interval training—one slow lap, one moderately paced lap, and one fast lap—over and over until he knew his physical limits. Under his father's tutelage, he learned how to time himself without a stopwatch; through sprinting drills, he acquired an ability to avoid being left behind in the home stretch. Over the course of his career, it would pay off.

When school ended, Johnny applied for a job at the British Canadian Co-operative Store in hopes of working outside making deliveries by horse and wagon. But there were few openings at the co-op, which had absorbed the staff from neighboring co-operatives that had closed because of the worsening situation in the coal and steel industry.

He worked one summer cleaning the ballast in cargo ships, and he acquired other part-time work around town, at the same time continuing to teach a Sunday-school class at the United Church in Florence. If his employment prospects were few, at least he had more time for running.

Johnny remembers the year 1923 well. In his first race that year, the three-mile Nate Nathansan event in Sydney, he shaved about four to five minutes off his previous time, placed second, and brought home a gold medal. His brother, Tom, entered the one-mile event that same day but quickly realized that his talents lay elsewhere. Johnny won his first race and his first trophy on July 2, at the three-mile Dominion Day road race in North Sydney. He ran the course in about 17 minutes. At the Antigonish Highland Games on August 23, he finished second to Westville's George Wright in a five-mile event. Already, the young runner had a following: Whenever his name appeared on a race program, a growing number of fans attended to cheer him on.

As he became more confident and experienced, Johnny's motivation changed. Little prizes were nothing, but gold medals and trophies symbolized accomplishment. He decided he would run until he did not enjoy it anymore.

His moment of triumph really arrived on Saturday, September 3, when he won his first race before a hometown crowd. Several hundred people lined the three-mile route, and Johnny broke the tape in fine style to win the Veteran's Silver Cup.

Despite his successes, however, the 17-year-old had a nagging feeling that he should be searching harder for a full-time job. Johnny knew that he would never be able to make a living running races, but he reasoned that he was still young, and his parents were encouraging him to continue. Perhaps, in some way, they were repaying him for the years he had spent working in the mine.

The grim employment climate in Cape Breton was worsening. In March, miners had reacted to a proposed slashing of wages by one-third, which caused the companies to back down temporarily. Twelve thousand striking miners left the pit at midnight on August 14; later that month, troops were sent into Glace Bay and other towns despite opposition from the mayors. The strike was settled, and the miners were forced to accept an 18-percent cut in take-home pay. The next February, all of the steelworkers at BESCO (British Empire Steel and Coal Company) in Sydney would strike for union recognition and against intolerable working conditions. Accepting a promise that their concerns would be addressed, the workers returned to their jobs. The demands were never fully met.

Times were hard, wages were low, and the lines were drawn between the companies and the unions, often splitting family loyalties. One of the few diversions was attending low-priced sporting events. Often for as little as 25 cents, one could watch ice hockey, sandlot baseball, cycling, harness racing, or road racing.

Athletic clubs and associations were well organized in the Maritimes in the early part of the 20th century. In most instances, they were an umbrella for a variety of community sports, sponsoring major events, building facilities, and helping to raise money so athletes like Johnny could compete outside their community. Road races were organized for every sort of holiday—Dominion Day, Labor Day, Thanksgiving weekend. Three- and five-mile events drew a large field of entries, while the 10-mile and 15-mile races were popular with the spectators.

It was therefore no surprise that the streets of the Whitney Pier district of Sydney were lined three and four deep with spectators on May 24, 1924. Johnny attempted a third time to win the Nathansan cup, but he placed second—again. It would be his only race that year.

Unable to find work in Sydney Mines, Johnny followed the route that many Cape Bretoners continue to travel, and he went to Ontario. On the railway in Cobalt, he, brother Tom, and friend Billy MacDonald found work. Johnny returned to Cape Breton in the spring of 1925 and found work in the blacksmith's shop at the Jubilee mine.

4 Boston Looms Large

On May 25, 1925, Johnny became the toast of Sydney and Sydney Mines when he finally won the Nathansan cup. After losing narrowly to popular local runners Reid Ross in 1923 and Mike Sullivan in 1924, Johnny redeemed himself that spring. With the crowd cheering and Ross on his tail, he completed the three miles in 15:18.

Johnny would earn the right to keep the trophy by racking up a second victory the following year. The prize was far from his last, but the hard-won cup became his most cherished. "Of the more than 40 trophies which I won during my all-too-brief career," he says, "none of them can compare with the Nate Nathansan cup."

There were more victories to come in 1925. A July 1 win in the one-mile event at Sydney's St. Thomas Sports Club was followed by a surprise victory in the annual Dartmouth Natal Day six-mile race, on August 6. In Baddeck 15 days later, he placed second in a one-mile race. By the time Johnny entered the Canadian Track and Field Championships held in Halifax, the sports fraternity was comparing him with the best middle-distance road runners in North America.

An exceptionally fine array of talent milled around Johnny on September 5 on the Wanderers' Club sports grounds: Jimmie Hawboldt, of Westville, Nova Scotia; Donald Young, of Halifax; and E. Paloheimo and G. Malmqvist, from Montreal, were among the nine runners entered in the five-mile championship race. The central-Canadian runners were ignorant of Johnny's exploding racing career, but by the end of the day, the name of the Sydney Mines runner was on everyone's lips. Johnny broke the tape in 26:50—one minute shy of F.G. Bellar's record of 25:31.8—and he went on to place third in the one-mile event.

The performance brought Johnny instant national recognition, but more importantly, he earned a promise from his father to sponsor an attempt at the 1926 Boston Marathon—if he won the upcoming 10-mile race in Halifax. Johnny was delighted: The *Herald* event was the top long-distance race in the province, and to win it was a milestone in any local runner's career. To win it on the first try would be extraordinary.

Shortly after returning to Sydney Mines, Johnny bumped into the manager of the co-operative store, who asked how he had done in the national championships. Not wanting to sound like a braggart, Johnny replied, "I won; I came first. How's that?" The manager, William Stewart, was obviously pleased and asked Johnny if he was still interested in a job with the company. Johnny accepted without hesitation, and it was agreed that he would start the next day. He started to fret immediately, however, about how to inform his boss at the coal mine that he was quitting, and he worried about finding the time to train for the Halifax race, only one month away. But he decided that his father would work it out.

As far as running was concerned, Johnny was feeling on top of the world. He told himself that with a lot of hard work and self-confidence, he would succeed. "Just you wait and see," he mused.

So, while Halifax and Boston loomed large, the rear end of the co-op's delivery horse loomed even larger as Johnny drove through Sydney Mines that first day on the new job. His work entailed cleaning and brushing Bobbie the horse and greasing the wagon before loading it with bags of potatoes, baskets and barrels of apples, and cases of canned goods. Johnny transported these items to the Florence co-op, where he helped the store clerks fill orders for private homes and small general stores. He could have used the co-op's Ford truck to deliver the larger orders, but he did not have a driver's permit. Well before 9 a.m., he was on the move again, making deliveries along the unpaved roads that wound their way through the colorful countryside and around Bras d'Or Lake. It was a rocky ride.

The well-known athlete soon became a popular traveller along the rural route, with children and adults alike greeting him or even tagging along. "There goes Johnny," the children could often be heard saying from the roadside.

Who would have picked this 19-year-old delivery boy as the athlete behind the face that was appearing in newspapers across the country? Who would have ventured a guess that Johnny would soon be supping with the political and social elite of Boston?

He worked hard to juggle the long days working for the co-op and meeting the demands of training. During the month before the *Herald* race, Johnny rose before the roosters crowed and ran an hour of short laps around the backyard track. Then after a quick wash or bath, he walked to the co-op stables to begin work at 7 a.m. After all deliveries were made, it usually took him about an hour to return home. No one remembers whether it was Johnny or Mr. Miles who came up with the idea of lengthening the horse's reins so that Johnny could run behind the wagon on the way home, but it does not matter: The scheme worked well. Johnny learned to ignore the puzzled bystanders who yelled, "Don't let him get away from you, Jack." The sight of Johnny puffing away while the horse set the pace soon lost its novelty but inspired many a local joke.

He lost count of the times he was delayed by the generosity of a farm family or lonely bachelor—all wanting to discuss his racing triumphs. After supper, there was more training to be done.

Leading up to Halifax, Johnny chalked up victories in Amherst, Antigonish, and New Glasgow.

On the eve of the Halifax race, word was spreading throughout Cape Breton sports circles that five-time winner Victor MacAulay, of Windsor, Nova Scotia, would be absent the next day. No one had believed MacAulay a year earlier when he said offhandedly that he would sit it out in 1925 to give someone else a chance.

Among those being touted by *Herald* sports editor J.E. "Gee" Ahern as possible successors to MacAulay were Silas McLellan, of Noel, Nova Scotia, who had finished second in 1924; Ronald O'Toole, a Newfoundlander who had placed third; and Westville's Jimmie Hawboldt, who had finished fourth the previous year. Two others were given outside chances of finishing in the top five: Jack Bell, a former winner of the *St. John's Telegram* race; and Johnny Miles, of Sydney Mines. Not one previous *Herald* winner was entered, and the field was wide open.

Since the *Herald* had inaugurated the modified marathon in 1907, only five people had won it. Hans Holmer, of Halifax, won the classic in its first two years; native Canadian "Big Chief" Mike Thomas, of Charlottetown, Prince Edward Island, was a three-time winner; and Alfred Rogers, a Dartmouthian of Wanderers' and Imperoyal club fame, won the race twice. No runner has surpassed MacAulay's record of five wins.

If Johnny were to win in Halifax, his chances of repeating in Boston were slim. The only person to have done that was Fred Cameron, of

Amherst, Nova Scotia, who won the Halifax race during Thanksgiving weekend 1909 and went on the next year to beat the reigning Boston champion, Canadian Henri Renaud.

Saturday, October 17, was not the best of days for Johnny to make his debut in the 10-mile event. It rained heavily all morning, and race officials considered postponing the 2 p.m. race because of a downpour a half-hour before starting time. Of the 36 official entries, 33 arrived, all opposing a postponement. The lineup was considered the finest ever assembled for the "Eastern Canadian Classic," but because the rain had muddied the streets of the newly altered course, few expected MacAulay's 1922 record of 54:29 to be beaten.

Number 6 on the program wore a pair of short black cutoffs in place of his usual knee-length running shorts. He also sported a white jersey with a dark stripe across the chest and a pair of the flat, inexpensive sneakers popular with runners of the era.

Somewhere in the rain-drenched crowd were Johnny's mother and father. The spectators applauded loudly at the crack of the starter's pistol, and the runners were on their way up Barrington Street, in the heart of the city.

For the first half-mile, the group bunched together. Then O'Toole, who had sailed through a stormy sea to get here, jumped into the lead at Richmond, in north-end Halifax. He kept an eye on Hawboldt and Johnny, and by the time he reached Africville, O'Toole had 20 yards on Johnny.

When some of the runners were forced to manoeuvre around a group of spectators, Johnny picked up a few yards going under the bridge at suburban Fairview. He then chased O'Toole up a short, steep hill. At Dutch Village, Hawboldt jumped ahead of Bell and several other runners who had been trailing the leaders. O'Toole was left with a five-yard advantage.

Like the Newton hills in Boston, Arm Hill in Halifax was a test that many hopefuls had failed, but O'Toole and Johnny climbed the hill together with seemingly little effort. The hundreds of spectators who stood at the sidelines cheered as the pack increased its pace coming into Oxford Street. Hawboldt had 100 yards on Bell, while McLellan moved into fifth spot.

Excitement grew as the leaders rounded South Street, where the final hill awaited. Like two racehorses, Johnny and O'Toole trotted up the steep incline, eyeing each other and sniffing victory. At Barrington Street,

Johnny moved into the centre of the road, and O'Toole opted to remain on the sidewalk. It was a costly mistake.

The wheels in Johnny's head were churning faster than his legs were as he opened up with a magnificent sprint that gave him a 15-yard lead. O'Toole's pace had been steady, but when he realized that the shouts were for Johnny, he sped up in an effort to catch the Cape Bretoner. Johnny would not be denied, making one last sprint to reach the tape in record time.

The time of 53:48.6 was so unbelievable, in fact, that officials decided to remeasure the rerouted course. It was found to be approximately 176 yards shy of 10 miles, so the times of Johnny and O'Toole were adjusted accordingly. Even with the new time, Johnny had shaved about seven seconds off the record.

For a brief period after the race, another minor controversy brewed. At the corner of Barrington and South streets—when O'Toole still held a 10-yard lead over Johnny—the faster-than-anticipated runners had had to compete with a streetcar turning the corner at the same time. Johnny had taken the initiative and run behind the streetcar for a short distance, on the side of the road. O'Toole did not notice. As he was about to pass an intersection leading onto Barrington Street, O'Toole found himself obstructed by the streetcar on one side and by a car on the other. The automobile backed up and allowed him to pass, but not before Johnny had gained a 50-foot lead. O'Toole resisted the suggestion, however, that he enter a protest, saying Johnny had won fairly.

The *Herald* later proclaimed the contest "the greatest long distance race ever held in Halifax." Ahern wrote that Johnny had showed "the speed of a [Fred] Cameron, the endurance of a [Hans] Holmer, and a heart characteristic of the athletes from his home country."

Hawboldt, Bell, and McLellan finished in that order. Ahern's predictions had been right on the button.

Johnny wasted little time in reminding his father of his promise, and the family returned to Sydney Mines convinced that Johnny could translate his 10-mile victory into a win in Boston. But Johnny had less than six months to build up his legs and his stamina for a full marathon, so he and his coach devised the most vigorous training schedule yet.

Every day—and most nights, too—Johnny put himself through a series of physical exercises, time laps, and long sprints behind the delivery wagon (and later a sleigh). Some evenings, returning to Sydney Mines from his delivery route, he drove past the Jubilee mine to pick up his father.

With Mr. Miles holding the reins, Johnny had the freedom to slow down or speed up at will, rather than at the pleasure of the horse. They encountered a few people who shouted "mild" obscenities at Mr. Miles, thinking him a cruel father punishing a wayward son.

When winter set in, Johnny began training at the tram tracks in town, usually the only place around that was regularly plowed of snow. Sometimes he even wore shorts, spreading a mixture of olive oil and wintergreen on his legs for protection. Slowly, he increased the length of his runs until he felt he could complete the 26-mile, 385-yard marathon.

At this time, Johnny was so popular with local children that a number of stories about him—some bordering on myth—began circulating around town. One story went that Johnny once told the police about a dog that had chased him and nipped at his ankle. Later, he enquired whether the police had found the beast. "Jack, my boy," replied Constable "Big" MacGregor, "you won't have to worry any longer. We found the dog and we shot it."

"You mean you found the one I reported?" Johnny supposedly asked.

"Well, we're not sure about that," said the policeman, "but we did find four dogs which were somewhat the same as the one you described, and since we didn't know which was the culprit, we shot them all."

Another story, probably more authentic, recalled how Johnny always brought home an unopened pay envelope from the coal mine and later from the co-operative, and gave it to his mother. Apparently, as a 12- or 13-year-old working at the mine, he received 25 cents a week for pocket money. Usually, he hung on to it, and before the week was out, his mother would ask for it back to buy some essential item for the family. During one two- or three-month period, however, Johnny managed to accumulate four quarters, which he put in a bank account, on someone's advice. He showed off the deposit book with pride. Shortly thereafter, a financial crisis arose, and Mrs. Miles asked for the money. Johnny pleaded but was forced to withdraw his lifetime savings. Expecting some interest on his deposit, he received only 98 cents, because of a two-cent service charge. Although Johnny is generous to a fault, that lesson in economics stuck with him, and he learned to manage his money wisely from then on.

What most demonstrated the respect that the neighborhood children had for Johnny, however, was their habit of imitating him. Andy MacDonald, a Sydney Mines native who is now a well-known author and character living in Port Elgin, New Brunswick, remembers that 15 to 20 youngsters often gathered at Sutherland's Corner to fall in behind Johnny during one of his runs. The lads included Stookie Herald, Red Carter, Chick Boyce, Billy "Fox" and Murray "Monkey" MacDonald, Warts, Dinty, and Snag. "We all loved Johnny very much," MacDonald says. Each child would imitate one of Johnny's mannerisms, from the way he shook his hands by his side to limber up to the way he counted his paces out loud. They often adopted his dress, too, which comprised a mishmash of clothing and, often, shorts in the winter. The characteristic that "puzzled [them] most" but was was easiest to copy was the "rag" wrapped around Johnny's right hand. It was not until years later that MacDonald realized the rag was actually a handkerchief that Johnny used to wipe sweat from his brow.

From these games grew an expression repeated even today by children who have heard of Johnny through older relatives. "When one of the kids who was running appeared to be taking himself too seriously," MacDonald recalls, "one of us would say, 'Hey, who do you think you are, Johnny Miles?'" Or boys boasted as they played, "I'm Johnny Miles."

"It wasn't only the running which made Miles a household word," says MacDonald. "It was just him."

Left to right: Eliza, Lena, Tom, Johnny, and John W. Miles.

Child coal miners.

Family home at Greener's Point.

Johnny delivering groceries for the co-op.

*With Jimmie Hawboldt (left) in
Halifax, 1925.*

Ronald O'Toole.

With some local children after Sunday school, 1926.

5 Facing the Challengers

In winning the 1926 Boston Marathon, Johnny became part of a Nova Scotia-Boston connection that had begun in 1898 with Ronald J. MacDonald. A native of Fraser's Grant, Antigonish County, MacDonald was a student at Boston College when he donned a pair of bicycle shoes and won the Boston Marathon in 2:42—the first Canadian to win it. He became a controversial member of the U.S. Olympic team at the 1900 Paris Olympics and a medical doctor. He was followed 12 years later by Fred Cameron, of Amherst, Nova Scotia, who outran newcomer Clarence DeMar in a time of 2:28.52. In the first 14 years of the marathon, Canadians won it five times.

The winners preceding Johnny had done it on a course measuring only 24.5 miles. In 1924, the course was apparently extended to meet the Olympic standard of 26 miles, 385 yards, and two years later, Johnny became the fastest Canadian ever to run "the Boston." Boston-area marathoner and frequent winner Clarence DeMar called Johnny's time of 2:25.4 "phenomenal." He explains in his book *Marathon* that the perform-ance caused officials to survey the course, and it was found to be 176 yards short. DeMar estimates that Johnny's recalculated time would have been 2:26.2, a time not surpassed until 1947, when South Korea's Yon Bok Suh completed the Boston Marathon in 2:25.39.

But the acclaim Johnny received in Boston was nothing compared with what awaited him in Nova Scotia. Hundreds of people turned out at railway stations across the province to greet the Mileses on their journey home. The widespread response has never been duplicated, and the closer the train edged towards Cape Breton, the more boisterous the receptions became.

Johnny was awarded silver cups in Stellarton and New Glasgow, Westville greeted him, and in the college town of Antigonish, the community turned out en masse. Cape Bretoners studying at St. Francis Xavier University took over the reception briefly, bands and student cheers filled the air, and the Highland Society presented Johnny with a gold watch and an honorary lifetime membership.

Newspapers carried extensive reports of the April 27 events: The *Sydney Record* ran six page-one articles under a banner headline. The Miles entourage included reporter Bill Cunningham, who was covering Johnny's homecoming for the *Boston Post.*

The Anglican Synod of Nova Scotia even passed a resolution in honor of the Presbyterian-United Church Sunday-school teacher: "Resolved that the appreciation of this Synod, now in session, be extended to John Miles for his single triumph in winning the Boston marathon, for 1926, for the fine Christian spirit manifested, and for the splendid impetus he has given to clean sports."

In brief speeches to the crowds, Johnny thanked everyone for the support he had received before and after the race, and he vowed to return to Boston in 1927.

When the Miles train came off the Canso ferry at Cape Breton Island, bagpipers led hundreds of Port Hawkesbury residents in giving the family a rousing welcome. Johnny's face was covered with a wide grin. At a civic reception, the small community added a silver cup to Johnny's collection.

As the train rolled along the last leg of its journey, a parade was forming in Johnny's home town. Pipers, drummers, a Salvation Army brass band, fire engines, trucks, cars, mounted police, sports teams, government officials, church congregations, and people of all sorts marched from the Sydney Mines town hall to the train station.

When Johnny and his parents stepped down from their sleeping car, the bands began to play, the people began to cheer, and the Marathon King and his companions were moved to tears. More than 5,000 people—twice the town's population—shouted, "Johnny! Johnny! Welcome home, Johnny!" A few, including his old friend Sam Keeling, shouted, "Jack, Jack!" Mayor Mike Dwyer welcomed the family and announced that a civic reception would follow at the town hall, at which point Johnny and the others were hoisted onto one of the fire trucks, and the parade returned to the hall. After handing Johnny a gold watch and a gold key to the town, the mayor said that the next day had been declared a public and school holiday.

Observed leaving the train that evening were little Andy MacDonald and his brother Murray, who had just experienced their first train ride, an 18-mile jaunt. Andy remembers that arrival as "one of the happiest moments in [my] young life, and my buddies', too, when Johnny was sitting on the Sydney Mines fire engine and a parade of cars following in celebration of his win."

Capping off the day was a spectacular fireworks display that could be seen for miles.

On "Johnny Miles Day," elementary-school and high-school students held their own parade, with Johnny as guest of honor. Concerts, sporting events, and a special reception hosted by Johnny's employer, the British Canadian Co-operative Society, all followed. The town response was unprecedented; never again would Sydney Mines give so much of itself to a local hero.

Celebrations also took place in Glace Bay, Dominion, and across the harbor in Sydney, where a fireworks demonstration, parades, concerts, and receptions were organized in Johnny's honor. He received a key to that city and was placed on the back of an open truck that bore a banner reading, "World's Greatest Marathoner."

With invitations continuing to pour in from all over Cape Breton, Johnny worried that he could lose his job because of the work he had been missing. But the co-op knew what a fine representative they had in Johnny: Everywhere he spoke, he praised the society for its support and understanding.

There was also the invitation, which Johnny accepted, to return to Boston on June 12 to participate in the DeMar Race in suburban Melrose. Stenroos and Jimmie Henigan would also be running, so Johnny knew that he could not rely on previous conditioning to win such a match. He picked up the training routine where he had left off and entered several provincial races to which he had been invited.

The challengers were already lining up to compete against the acclaimed Boston Marathon champion.

He responded by winning three races in quick succession. His first event after Boston was the three-mile Nathansan race in Sydney, which he won a second time to become owner of the cup. A few days later, on May 31, he won a six-mile race in North Sydney against a three-man relay team consisting of Donald McLeod, Douglas Angel, and Donald Robin. He also won a five-mile event on June 2 in Stellarton.

The next day, Johnny was expected to go head to head with Jimmie Hawboldt for the Maritime 10-mile title, in Amherst, Nova Scotia. It was the Amherst Athletic Association's annual track and field day, and a crowd in excess of 2,000 gave Johnny a tremendous ovation before the race as Mayor H.D. Biden presented him with a cup and a key to the town. The track was spongy and the winds strong, but Johnny completed the 10 miles in 56:26, a few hundred yards ahead of Hawboldt, who had shadowed his rival for the first six miles. It would not be the last close race between these two Nova Scotia favorites.

With the co-op's blessing, Johnny and his parents returned to Boston a few days before the Melrose invitational. There, they attended a series of receptions in their honor, and Melrose treated them to a torchlit parade and a luncheon, where 20-year-old Johnny was introduced as "perhaps the greatest long-distance runner the world has ever known." Little did the Mileses know that an event like this one would be Johnny's downfall on the day of the race.

Johnny recalls that when a business organization invited him to a noon luncheon to be held on race day, he considered declining but attended out of politeness. Once there, the rich food and pastries were too tempting for him to pass up. "When the race started," he says, "I had a sick, overloaded feeling, and I guess I just ran out of gas."

The weather that day was also working against him: Johnny was known as a cold-weather runner, and the sun was scorching in Melrose. Among the crowd was Peter Campbell—who had helped organize the Mileses' first Boston trip—and he witnessed Johnny and Stenroos running in close quarters near the six-mile mark, where Johnny suddenly collapsed. Concern rippled through the crowd. Johnny was unable to finish because of stomach cramps, and Stenroos went on to win.

Afterwards, Mr. Miles told reporters that Johnny's poor showing had been "purely an accident." He assured everyone that his son was not discouraged and was, in fact, looking forward to a return match against Stenroos and DeMar. Both runners had been invited to the July 1 10-mile event on the Exhibition Grounds in Halifax.

In Nova Scotia's capital, the race sponsor, the Crescents' Athletic Club, was pulling out all of the stops in order to build interest in the Dominion Day race. It was reported that track rivals Jimmie Henigan and Johnny Miles would be running, and a later bulletin indicated that DeMar had agreed to come, too. This was retracted when DeMar announced that he had other commitments. Stenroos had returned to Finland. To top it off, July 1—Canada's birthday—would be declared "Johnny Miles Day" in

Halifax. Both Johnny and Henigan were to be honored by civic and provincial government officials.

And so it happened that on race day, more than 7,000 people—4,000 more than had been anticipated—crammed the Exhibition Grounds. As was common at the time, the track and field events were punctuated by a horse race—this time one of the most hotly contested light-harness racing events in years. Vera Gratton, a popular horse driven by owner Frank Adams, broke a 20-year track record for a one-mile event.

The 10-mile foot race featured 10 starters, but it was truly a Miles-Henigan contest. Henigan set the pace, while Johnny was content to maintain a distance. Just before the finish, Johnny sprinted to break through the tape at 54:14.4. Silas McLellan finished third.

Instead of competing in Halifax, Jimmie Hawboldt ran and won a five-mile contest that day in his home town of Westville. A popular runner with an enviable record, Hawboldt trained whenever he had time away from the coal mine, and it was not unusual for him to leave work and go directly to a race. Although never tempted to make a grab for the Boston prize, he was determined to get a leg up on Johnny's success. He would have his chance three weeks later in Antigonish.

Johnny was favored to continue his winning ways at the July 21 Highland Games. Established in 1861, the Antigonish Highland Society organized a set of games considered most like the original Highland Games in Scotland. Of the 4,000 or so people in the grandstands that day, the loudest component seemed to support Hawboldt, who was primed for the five-mile track event.

The starter fired his pistol, and Hawboldt moved quickly ahead of the seven other entrants. Johnny dogged the leader's heels for the first 19 laps and then, at the beginning of the 20th lap, surged ahead. He appeared to be in control of the race. But on the back stretch, Hawboldt regained the lead, maintaining it to the finish and breaking the tape to a standing ovation. His time was 29:35. Angus MacDonald, of Antigonish, placed third.

Almost immediately, a major dispute loomed. Johnny questioned the officials for not having used a flag or other device to signal the start of the final lap. He said that he had believed there was one more lap to go, until he saw Hawboldt finish and the crowd go wild. The race committee ruled that because it was not usual to give such a signal in the games, the results stood. A disappointed Johnny accepted their decision without further comment.

In Stellarton, Pictou Landing, Westville, and New Glasgow—throughout Hawboldt's home area—Hawboldt became the new hero of the people. Member of Parliament for Pictou, Tom Cantley, sent Hawboldt a telegram, and the runner received a letter from a man who was obviously not a fan of Johnny Miles. Edison Cummings—who worked for the Maritime Coal, Railway and Power Company at Joggins—wrote on company stationery, "Hello old man. Allow me to congratulate you on yesterday's feat, gad Jim, that tickled me. I suppose I can say with the rest of the dopesters that *I told you so,* well I was honest in my predictions. I was sorry to see in the *Herald,* that Johnny gave such an excuse as not knowing it was the last lap, thot [*sic*] it was the [19]th. I hardly credit the World Champion, is it right? I sincerely hope he is a better sport than that."

Two days after his loss to Hawboldt, Johnny met Henigan again in an exhibition 10-mile run in Yarmouth. Johnny recorded another win for the scrapbook, which Mr. Miles and his son Tom kept.

He was back in Massachusetts on August 7 for the 73rd annual Caledonia Games at West Roxbury. The lineup was billed as the most impressive one ever to oppose Johnny at a distance of 15 miles: DeMar, Henigan, and "Whitey" Michelson, of New York. But driving rain forced many of the spectators out of the stands, and the track became a sea of mud.

Consistent with past performances, Michelson took the lead and held it for 12 miles, then appeared to weaken. At the 13-mile mark, Johnny sensed the effect the rain was having on Michelson and jumped to the front of the pack, setting an unfaltering pace. Henigan and DeMar also overtook Michelson—who would finish fourth—but they were lapped by the Cape Bretoner. Sprinting to the tape with a 300-yard lead, Johnny received an enthusiastic reaction from the fans who had braved the rain. His time was 1:33.12.4. Henigan and DeMar, more than a lap behind, crossed the finish line in that order.

It was an amazing performance by Johnny, who showed no sign of being winded. Who knows what his time may have been if conditions had been better? He had more than compensated for the Melrose race he could not complete.

Johnny followed with a relatively poor fourth-place finish in a 10-mile track event on August 13 in Sydney, but he went on to win four consecutive five-mile races: in Kentville, in the Annapolis Valley, where he again topped Henigan, in Pictou, in Moncton, New Brunswick, and in New Glasgow. He was crowned Maritime five-mile champion after the September 6 win in Moncton, where he won with a time of 27:11.2.

Another showdown with Hawboldt took place on September 11, in Hawboldt's home town. The vocal Westville fans watched spellbound as Hawboldt and Johnny ran almost as one for most of the five miles. A last-minute burst of speed gave Hawboldt a dramatic victory—by less than 20 feet.

Johnny regained the advantage with an even-closer victory on September 24. With the Prince Edward Island Exhibition and a continuous rain as backdrop, Johnny and Hawboldt exchanged the lead several times during the five-mile race before Johnny got the jump and won by 15 feet.

Then came a special 10-mile event staged October 6 at the trotting park in Sydney. Hawboldt and Johnny thrilled an overflow crowd of 6,000 horse-racing enthusiasts by battling in another close contest. Despite a 20-knot southwest wind, Johnny outran Hawboldt by about 400 yards and completed the 10 miles in 57:19.4. The only other runner, North Sydney's Don McLeod, was not able to make up the third of a lap that separated him from Johnny.

All of this was just a prelude to the greatest 10-mile contest Nova Scotia had ever seen. It was the popular modified marathon in Halifax, slated for October 23, and the 46 runners were considered the most formidable collection of athletes ever assembled in the Maritimes. Among them were Clarence DeMar, four-time winner of the Boston Marathon; Silas McLellan, always a threat; Newfoundlander Ronald O'Toole, who was seeking a first win on Canadian soil; Charles Snell, of Toronto's Gladstone Athletic Club; Jimmie Hawboldt; and Johnny, representing the Sydney Athletic Association with Reid Ross, John N. MacDonald, and Billy B. Hunter.

On the morning of the race, Johnny confided to a reporter that he was "in grand shape" and ready to do battle. "I expect to win, of course, but the field is a strong one and I realize I have my work cut out for me," he was quoted as saying. "There are a dozen runners here today who are dangerous."

DeMar, who had travelled by ship from Boston to Yarmouth, and then by train, had overcome a bout of seasickness and was feeling confident. Snell was rated as one of the best middle-distance runners in his part of the country, and the eight-member Newfoundland contingent was a determined bunch. Hawboldt was also anxious to win.

As the pack set off at 1:20 p.m., a pleasant midday sun was taking some of the nip out of the autumn air. About 50 minutes later, the large crowd was surprised to see the five-foot three-inch, 108-pound Snell entering the gates of the track as the leader. Reports had filtered back that Johnny appeared sluggish. Snell was halfway around the track by the time the second runner entered the gates—to a tumultuous reception. But Johnny could not make up the distance, and Snell won in 54:14.8. Johnny was 39 seconds behind.

The greatest ovation seemed to be reserved for DeMar, a printer and Sunday-school teacher who would compete for more than 49 years, until shortly before his death in 1958. On his heels and a close fourth was O'Toole. Hawboldt finished sixth.

The intensity of the past few months was beginning to take its toll on Johnny. Since winning in Boston in April, he had competed in 19 races, winning 14 of them, placing second three times, third one time, and failing to complete a race on one occasion. He had also made a spate of public appearances. Winter was approaching, a good time to slow down and pay more attention to his job and to other concerns.

On October 30, Johnny turned 21, the legal drinking age, but he had no interest in joining his co-workers at the beer parlor. He was even featured in the textbook *Success and Health,* which was used in Nova Scotia and Quebec schools at the time. In a section entitled "Alcohol and Drugs Not Your Friends," Johnny's photograph was published along with a few words of advice. "One of Canada's best marathoners" told students, "To be a successful athlete, you must think clean, live clean and obey the laws of nature."

Johnny's priorities differed from those of most of his friends. While his chums dated, planned for the future, married and raised children, Johnny dated only occasionally. Most of the women in his life were co-workers or acquaintances from the church. He was a religious man, and his ties with the church were strong. Publications such as the *Palm Branch,* issued by the United Church of Canada's Women's Society, printed articles about Johnny and his dedication to his faith. When his Sunday-school class presented him with a Bible after his Boston victory, the event was noted in the local newspaper.

Johnny was a bright light for his home town during its period of pain and transition. Like other mining towns, Sydney Mines was changing physically and politically. The coal-company stores had disappeared after angry miners had burned them down in 1925; and while the old system of being indebted to the companies was certainly not mourned, veteran miners missed the warm, social atmosphere around the potbellied stove.

The stores' demise may have given a boost to the co-operative society, but there was little cash in the miners' pockets. Most were working only three or four days per week.

6 Defending the Title

Nineteen twenty-six had been busy, but the following year was even busier. For Johnny, 1927 was a year of decision-making and achievement, of controversy and disappointment. He would change addresses and exchange his co-op delivery wagon for an International Harvester freight cart.

In the spring of 1927, as the snow melted and the roads muddied, the thoughts of sportswriters turned to running. Local newspapers reviewed Johnny's performance over the past year and assessed his chances of winning again in Boston. *Herald* sports editor Gee Ahern saw that a fund was established for the Mileses' return to Boston. Newspapers such as the *Sydney Record* and the Halifax *Chronicle* joined in the collection campaign with reports listing the donations, which arrived from throughout the Maritimes, from other parts of Canada, and from the United States. Churches, sports clubs, schools, town councils, students, and workers all added their names to the growing list.

Still reeling from poor economic times, the Town of North Sydney contributed $434. From Florence came a cheque for $50, the proceeds of a community dance. Collections were organized among patients and staff at hospitals, in the retail shops, and in mines and workshops. People stopped Johnny along his delivery route and made cash donations. Sports associations that had benefited from Johnny's fame in the form of gate receipts but that were slow to contribute were chastised in the papers, and their purse strings loosened.

Johnny recollects that he received more than $1,500. Such community response was usually reserved for times of adversity or tragedy, and seldom had an individual athlete received such financial support.

The Yarmouth Steamship Company, on the other tip of Nova Scotia, offered Johnny and his parents free passage to Boston. This news set in motion widespread plans to receive the family along the route, from one end of the province to the other.

Relieved that others were handling the details of the trip, Johnny concentrated on his race strategy: He was determined to live up to the confidence that was being displayed in him. One of the last things he and his father did was prepare a new pair of running shoes.

From time to time during the winter, the two of them had discussed what impact lightweight shoes would have on Johnny's time. They concluded that they could reduce his 1926 record by 10 minutes, so Mr. Miles took a straight razor and trimmed the soles of the shoes so thin that Johnny could almost feel the kitchen linoleum beneath his feet. His father suggested that heavy woolen socks would provide an adequate cushion. Fearing that information about their secret weapon would leak out, expecting sure victory, and dreaming of a revolution in the running-shoe industry, the athlete and coach kept the shoes under wraps until race day.

On April 4, with farewell greetings and bagpipe music ringing in their ears, Johnny and his parents boarded the train for Yarmouth. Mrs. Miles wore a stylish fur coat, Mr. Miles sported a three-piece, blue-serge suit, and Johnny was attired in a blue shirt and tie, a Wanderers' Club sweater, and a snappy grey-tweed suit. Ahern wrote that Johnny was "a strong rival for the present-day matinee idols."

Along the route, people came out of their farmhouses and wandered down streets to wish them Godspeed. On to Truro, through the Annapolis Valley, along the South Shore to Yarmouth, the Mileses were heaped with warm greetings. Spontaneous receptions, speeches, cash purses, gold pieces, and more than enough advice were all offered Johnny.

When the Dominion Atlantic Railway train pulled into Yarmouth, the size of the welcoming crowd overwhelmed the family. Kiwanis Club members escorted them in a small cavalcade to Wagner's Dining Room, where the mayor, other officials, and reporters waited. The mayor handed the steamship tickets over to Johnny, and the YMCA and a Zion church Sunday-school class gave him a donation.

When the Mileses finally boarded the *Prince Arthur*, they encountered curious passengers who had heard that the marathon champion would be among them. Johnny was no longer the unknown who had travelled to

Boston a year earlier: His photograph had appeared in almost every major newspaper in North America and even on the front page of a Helsinki, Finland, paper. A race horse and a boat even bore his name.

He spent a lot of time during that voyage up on the deck gazing out into the water. Johnny enjoyed those moments away from the crowds. The past 12 months had been a wonderful experience for the young man from a small town, but as the ship steamed into Boston, the expectations of his country lay heavily on his mind.

Following the 1926 victory, one sportswriter had suggested that Johnny was a "worthy successor to Pheidippides," the legendary Athenian runner. Another wrote, "Miles has carved for himself a niche in the Athletic Hall of Immortals."

Unknown to Johnny and his parents, a minor drama was unfolding in Boston. One week before, it had been discovered that the course was 176 yards shy of the official distance of 26 miles, 385 yards, and adjustments had to be made. While the official explanation was that organizers had checked the route because Olympic officials were considering reducing that marathon to 25 miles, the reaction in Nova Scotia and elsewhere was less than positive. One newspaper suggested that it was an effort to discredit Johnny and his record. Others thought it was a way to dishearten the reigning champion.

On the day before the 1926 marathon, Albin Stenroos had stated publicly that the course was not standard length. He questioned the method by which it had been measured, adding that Finnish marathons were "measured with a tape." After crossing the finish line four minutes behind the victorious Johnny, Stenroos conceded that the course was "perhaps long enough."

To assure a precise remeasuring of the course, Professor Edward Sheiry, of the Massachusetts Institute of Technology's engineering department, plus six BAA officials, drove the route and decided that the starting point would have to be moved 176 yards towards the centre of Hopkinton. The finish line would remain adjacent to the BAA clubhouse on Exeter Street. The asphalt roads had also been recently resurfaced, which worried the runners.

While it was decided that the three previously established times and Johnny's 1926 record would stand—the course having been remeasured once before, in 1924—it was also announced that the winner of the 1927 event would be credited with setting the first record for the official distance.

As he arrived in Boston and was escorted to the Commonwealth Hotel, Johnny was unbothered by these events, actually appearing excited about the prospects of a new challenge. Thanks to the generosity of the folks back home, he was able to afford more luxurious accommodation this time around. He stayed in the hotel for a few days, using his free time to reacquaint himself with the city. Shortly before the Patriot's Day race, the family moved to the Somerset Hotel, as guests of the Cape Breton Club.

Johnny was the odds-on favorite of the bookmakers, and there were reports of several lotteries in progress. Apparently, various betting possibilities have long been associated with the race, and from time to time, people have speculated about attempts to fix the results. While never proven, charges surrounding the 1901 drugging of Antigonish native Ronald J. MacDonald, the first Canadian to win the marathon, caused a few ripples. In 1900, betting between the followers of the Canadian and U.S. competitors almost resulted in bloodshed.

As the race drew closer, Johnny's mind was filled with thoughts of his secret weapon. He modestly suggested to the media that despite the addition of 176 yards to the course, he would clip at least 40 seconds off his record.

DeMar, mindful of Johnny's successes during the past year, picked Johnny to repeat and said that he would place second. A record number of entries was forecast, including several new challengers. Clifford Bricker, of Galt, Ontario, was appearing for the first time; and DeMar picked him to finish among the first five. Also picking Johnny to win was the *Boston Post's* Bill Cunningham, who had written glowing articles about Johnny's 1926 win and reception in Cape Breton.

Johnny continued to exude a confidence that seemed to confirm all of the positive predictions that were being made about him. His weight was down to 128, and his legs were as supple as ever. He had stuck to a fixed diet and had even brought his own bread with him—24 loaves the co-operative baker had prepared in tightly sealed tins.

Shortly before noon on April 19, 164 runners assembled under a scorching sun in the centre of Hopkinton, their number reduced from the more than 200 who had registered. The weather was already taking its toll. Johnny changed into his special running shoes. Considering the lengths to which local reporters went for material, it was indeed surprising that the secret had not leaked out.

At the sound of the starter's pistol, DeMar edged his way to the front of the pack. Wearing number 32, Johnny held back at the beginning and planned to surge forward later. But the heat, in the high 80s, had a greater effect on him than he had anticipated, and he soon felt weak and nauseated. He noticed that DeMar and Koski were increasing their pace, but he seemed incapable of matching them.

Then, as if he had been hit by a stray bullet, a look of horror came over his face. Johnny could feel the heat of the asphalt through the soles of his sneakers and, before long, realized that black tar was seeping into his shoes, making his feet more than a little slippery inside the woolen socks. The tar was sticking to his heels, making running very difficult. Soon other runners were passing him, and he realized that unless he overcame this painful problem, he would not be able to finish.

The hot, sticky tar started to burn Johnny's toes and the soles of his feet, blisters began to form, and soon, a mixture of blood and black muck was oozing out of the upper part of his sneakers. The pain was excruciating, and Johnny bit into his cheek, hoping that it would pass. But this was different than a stitch in the side or a momentary loss of breath. Each step was taking a greater toll, and Johnny was no longer capable of concentrating on the race. His mind was consumed by the damage he was doing to his feet.

Somewhere between the fourth and seventh mile, Johnny ignored the exhortations of onlookers and made a choice that would haunt him for years. As one of the newspaper vehicles came alongside, he jumped onto its running board and was automatically disqualified. The thought of his father and mother waiting at the finish line bothered him but not nearly so much as the pain in his feet, which were raw to the touch. As the vehicle passed dozens of runners who had already dropped out, Johnny asked to be taken to his hotel.

DeMar, who was more comfortable running under such conditions, managed to complete the race in a winning time eight minutes slower than Johnny's year-old record. Koski placed second, another four minutes behind DeMar; and perennial entry Bill Kennedy, the 1917 title holder, placed third. Bricker ran fourth.

DeMar later wrote of the 1927 race in *Marathon*. He said that he was "racing against Miles that day. In all my other marathons I've raced against time but this race it was Miles, the fastest runner ever. I just wouldn't let Miles keep the lead but would spurt ahead every quarter mile. It was hot— so hot that the tar was like flypaper in places. So, I wasn't surprised that before Natick, Miles, from the frozen North, quit. In trimming Miles I had become tired—and I still had twenty miles to go."

More than 100 runners were forced to the sidelines because of the heat and the road conditions, but it was Johnny's exit that elicited the near-unanimous condemnation of the media. A virulent attack by Bill Cunningham brought tears to Johnny's eyes. The April 20 article in the *Post* said that Johnny had quit without a fight, and Cunningham suggested that this was no way for a champion to perform. "That isn't the way championships pass," he wrote. "Johnny Miles should have finished ... if he had to crawl across the finish line on his hands and knees, after the hour of midnight with his bleeding feet wrapped in newspapers."

Johnny was angry with Cunningham, who knew that Johnny was no quitter, and he was angry with himself for going along with the super-shoe scheme. Yet he promised the Boston press that "there are other days coming." When the day did come two years later, Cunningham would be forced to eat his words. (The curious thing about the entire crazy shoe plan was that it remained a secret until 1929, when Johnny revealed the story. He wrote about the incident years later for *Canadian Runner* magazine.)

Mr. Miles seemed dismayed, but he defended his son's actions by suggesting, "He didn't know what he was doing." He went on to say that Johnny had been under a strain because of the great expectations that others had placed on him. "I feel he's losing confidence," Mr. Miles said. This remark made Johnny uncharacteristically upset: He rejected the idea and vowed to return, if not the following year, then in 1929.

In Canada, and particularly in Nova Scotia, the news was met with widespread disappointment, but Johnny received support from many quarters. In the Halifax *Herald,* Gee Ahern noted that other champion marathoners had dropped out of races, including Tom Longboat, who had given up in an Olympics, and Frank Zuna, a former Boston Marathon winner who had quit this time long before Johnny had. "Personally, we still believe Miles to be the world's leading marathoner," Ahern wrote, "and Nova Scotia should not be too ready to say 'Johnny Miles is through,' for he is only starting."

The New York Times, mentioning that more than 100 runners had been forced to withdraw, said Johnny was "no exception."

After the Boston fiasco, one of the few invitations Johnny received to receptions in that city came from the Cape Breton Club, and true to the island spirit, the Mileses were welcomed warmly on returning to Sydney Mines. Anxious to shake off his disappointment, Johnny went back to work driving the delivery wagon for the co-op.

With the aid of soothing foot baths from his mother and words of encouragement from his father, he was soon back in training. He needed a win against a top-rate field in order to restore his confidence—a 15-mile race slated for Victoria Day on Glace Bay's Black Diamond Race Track was just the thing. Two of the three best American marathoners—DeMar and Henigan—had agreed to come, while Whitey Michelson declined the invitation.

The Glace Bay crowd was thrilled when popular Sydney runner Reid Ross led the field for most of the first 12 miles. But blistered feet then slowed Ross, who was attempting 15 miles for the first time, and he eventually settled for fourth place. Matching Ross' pace for most of the distance was Henigan, who finished second, about 300 yards behind the winner. Johnny, holding back until the end, took the lead from Henigan at the 13-mile point. The "Pride of Cape Breton," as the *Herald* had called him, brought the 9,000 spectators to their feet.

Although the day was colder than Johnny preferred—with a 30-mile-an-hour northwest wind making the going tough—Johnny was clocked at a very respectable 1:25.7.5. Silas McLellan took third, and DeMar finished a disappointing sixth.

Later that month, on May 30, Johnny came third in a full marathon in Buffalo, New York, before an estimated crowd of 100,000 people. A few weeks later, in a 10-mile thriller in Halifax, he solidified his regained reputation and avenged his loss to Snell the year before. From the second-mile mark, until they began running shoulder to shoulder at the end of mile number four, Snell led Johnny and looked as if he was going to win again. By the end of the sixth mile, they had both lapped McLellan and Ray Hamilton. Throughout the race, Snell took lots of water; but Johnny waited until the seven-mile mark before accepting a wet sponge from his father.

Going into the ninth mile, Johnny surged ahead of Snell with a well-timed sprint, moving Halifax *Chronicle* reporter Bob Anderson to write, "With great strides, piston-like in their regularity, Johnny Miles—son of Cape Breton and holder of the world's marathon record, won the ten-mile running race...."

It was said that 1,700 fans had jumped over the fence of the Wanderers' Grounds to see the race.

After Halifax, Johnny's faith in himself was fully restored. One evening in early July, he drove Bobbie the horse into the co-op stable for the last time, packed a small club bag, and boarded a train for Hamilton, Ontario. Canadian officials had approached Johnny after his 1926 record-breaking win in Boston and suggested he try out for the 1928 Olympics. He was going to take them up on it.

7 The Road to the Olympics

From 1890 until the end of World War II, Hamilton claimed the enviable reputation of being track and field capital of eastern Canada. It was a well-deserved title, reaching a high point in the mid-1920s. Several athletic clubs with a rich history in major track events were attracting scores of aspiring runners from across the country. These clubs offered a high calibre of coaching and training programs and sweetened the pot with an abundance of sports facilities.

From the turn of the century, middle- and long-distance runners, wearing the colors of these athletic clubs, carved a place for Hamilton in the world sports spotlight. Jack Caffery, of the St. Patrick's Athletic Club, won the Boston Marathon in 1900 and 1901. Bill Sherring, of the same club, won the marathon event at the 1906 "unofficial" Olympics in Athens. Another local runner, James Duffy, won the Boston Marathon in 1914.

This was the atmosphere into which Johnny strode when he arrived on July 7, 1927, to compete in the marathon trials hosted by the Hamilton Olympic Athletic Club. Almost immediately, he found himself in a sea of long-distance runners with established reputations in the 10,000-metre and marathon competitions, including future members of the 1928 Olympic team: Cliff Bricker, Harold Webster, of Hamilton, Guelph's Johnny Cuthbert, and Percy Wyer and Charles Snell, of Toronto. He also met the person who would be the track and field coach at the 1928 Amsterdam Olympics, Captain J. Cornelius. Johnny was impressed with the training facilities, which were vastly superior to anything he had seen in Nova Scotia.

During the marathon trials, Bricker set a new Canadian record of 2:51.46. Johnny did not run well—placing ninth with a time of 3:23.28—so his coach suggested that he stay in Hamilton for further training.

As much as the idea appealed to him, Johnny had to think about his job in Sydney Mines and about his parents and family, whom he missed very much. It was the kind of dilemma he had always relied on his father to resolve. He knew that in order to stay in Hamilton, he would have to find a job there. One part of him realized that he might never have this opportunity again, but another felt guilty about leaving the people who had done so much for him.

He came up with a solution: He would stay in Hamilton and, after finding a job, would invite his family to give up everything and move there, too. He mailed a letter home with this suggestion but soon realized that he had been a bit selfish, and perhaps premature. He awaited the reply, imagining how upset his mother was going to be.

To his surprise, neither his mother nor his father thought it was a crazy idea. "Get a job, son, and then we'll talk about it some more," they responded.

Meanwhile, Johnny had heard that the International Harvester plant in town was hiring laborers and that he might have a chance at acquiring temporary employment. Bobby Robinson, sports editor for the *Hamilton Spectator*, offered to put in a good word with the plant manager.

On October 4, Johnny began working in the fibre and twine division as a trucker. When he inquired what the salary was, the manager asked what his weekly pay had been in Cape Breton. "Twenty-two dollars and 50 cents, sir," Johnny replied confidently. "Fine," said the manager, "we'll match it." Johnny wrote a letter of resignation to his former boss at the co-op.

Compared with workdays at the co-operative, which could stretch as long as 12 hours, Johnny's new eight-hour shift at Harvester was terrific, because it left him with more time for training. Each evening after work, he left the room he had rented at the YMCA on James Street South and ran seven to 10 miles along the highway, as far as the jam factory in Fruitland. Often, he repeated this run before going to work in the morning.

Among the pleasures he derived from his training routine were massages by John Beer, who operated the YMCA's massage room. For the sum of three dollars, Johnny was treated to a vigorous half-hour rubdown. Beer was a professional, and he helped Johnny become more aware of every muscle and nerve in his body.

The Cape Breton boy was terribly homesick, however, so he was overjoyed when his family consented to move to Hamilton. His only hope was that everything would work out for them and that his brother and his father would find suitable jobs.

On October 31, one day after Johnny's 22nd birthday, Mr. and Mrs. Miles, daughters Lena and Lillian, and son Tom climbed into the family car—an Oakland Lando sedan they had purchased in Boston in 1927—and followed Johnny to Ontario. It was not easy to leave the neighbors and friends they had known for 21 years. They had helped one another, cared for each other's children, and comforted one another in times of strain and sorrow. As well, Mr. Miles had been reluctant to give up his position teaching a course to miners; but new conflicts were arising between government and the unions, and it was probably a good time to leave.

When people in Sydney Mines learned that the Mileses were planning to move, they inundated the family with best wishes and passed on greetings to their most-famous member. In some ways, the entire clan had become special, even before Johnny was acclaimed Marathon King.

His parents and siblings had missed Johnny more than they were ready to admit. So much of their free time during the past few years had been taken up with his racing career that they believed he needed them as much as they needed him.

The Mileses spent the first night on the road in St. Peters, Cape Breton, and the next day took the Strait of Canso ferry for the last time. Rather than drive directly to Hamilton, they made a detour to Halifax to watch Johnny run the full marathon on November 7 against a top-flight field that included Clarence DeMar and Billy Taylor, a repeat winner of the Nathansan cup.

In a cold rain, the family cheered on their favorite runner as DeMar dogged Johnny's heels for the first 15 miles. Long after Johnny broke the tape in 2:40.29.2, a chilled and tired DeMar crossed the finish line in 10th position for a time of 3:30—one of the poorest showings of his career. He had walked most of the last 10 miles. Taylor finished second.

Johnny returned to Hamilton by train, and the family continued its road trip. Tom, who was 19 at the time, remembers the journey as being far from pleasurable. "I don't think we missed a day when we didn't have at least one tire blow-out," he says. "We came across bridges washed out and, in Quebec, snowstorms. Going through the old town in Quebec City, we got halfway up a steep hill and then slipped all the way back down on the ice."

Shortly after the family left Sydney Mines, 12-year-old Lillian broke out in a red rash, thought to be a nervous reaction to leaving her friends behind but later found to be measles. From then on, Lillian stayed in the car when the family stopped at a roadside cafe or restaurant. By the time she reached Hamilton, she was sick of cold sandwiches and messy desserts.

On the outskirts of the city the evening of November 12, the Oakland Lando was suddenly surrounded by heavy fog, so Tom suggested that they stop at a hardware store to purchase a flashlight. Johnny laughs as he recounts the story of his father walking in front of the car, shining the light, as Tom drove "at a snail's pace," finally arriving on his doorstep at the James Street YMCA. "They arrived looking rather tired," Johnny recalls. "I remember Tom muttering something about the fog, and I wasn't paying much attention to what he was saying, because I was so taken with the way they were dressed. All five of them were wearing coveralls, which they thought were quite practical for travelling. They looked like a bunch of country folk from the hills of Arkansas. They were some sight."

At first, the Mileses stayed at a small hotel on King Street, but they soon heard of a new house for sale on Balsam Avenue. It was exactly what they wanted, and, before long, they were settled at 146 Balsam Avenue North, directly opposite Hamilton Civic Stadium, in Scott Park. Johnny moved in with them.

Mr. Miles found a job with the City of Hamilton, building sewers— he would later work as a stationery engineer with a lithograph company— and soon he and Johnny were back to a strict training routine. From the loft window on the third floor, he clocked Johnny as he sped around the stadium track. Usually, Johnny ran in the evening after the stadium was closed. He would scale the high fence using a two-by-four-inch piece of wood as a ladder and run in the dark under the light of the moon.

Johnny continued to train at the YMCA and receive massages there, and he was a member of the Hamilton Olympic Athletic Club. He also kept up his road work, even after winter set in.

His work trucking materials from the freight elevator to the shop floor was not scintillating, but Harvester was generous in providing time off for specialized training and competitions. Before long, Johnny was given the job of oiling machines on the same floor. The pay remained the same.

Although Johnny had his sights set that winter on a return to Boston in April, his Olympic coach instructed him to stay home. The team did not want to take a chance on Johnny injuring himself or peaking too soon. Cliff Bricker was also advised to skip Boston and get in shape for Amsterdam. Johnny accepted the coach's dictate, even though his absence in Boston could have been misinterpreted. He still felt a sense of having let people down in 1927, and he wanted to restore his reputation. Yet doing well at the Olympics was a higher priority.

Canada, without Johnny, was still well represented at the 32nd running of the Boston classic: 24 runners, mostly from Nova Scotia and Ontario, arrived to compete. A favorite among the Canadian contingent was Billy Reynolds, emerging as one of Canada's leading runners in the 10,000-metre. Reynolds had outrun Canada's best in the 1928 Good Friday 15-mile event in Toronto. Silas McLellan, from Hants County, Nova Scotia, was back in Boston, along with Billy Taylor, from Sydney Mines, Hector Corkum, from Lunenburg, Donald Young, from Halifax, and Alfred Rodgers, from Dartmouth. Montreal native and 1915 Boston winner Edouard Fabre was also entered. But it was DeMar all the way, setting a course record for the second consecutive year, in a time of 2:37.7. McLellan was the top Canadian, placing 10th.

Johnny followed the race results from his home in Hamilton. For now, there was the Canadian Track and Field Championships—also designated the Olympic trials—set for June 30 to July 2, in Hamilton.

Despite a highly criticized performance in the Toronto 15-mile race on Good Friday, in which he led but was forced to his knees and then to the sidelines by a stitch, Johnny was determined to compete in the 10,000-metre trials in hopes of qualifying to run this distance in Amsterdam, in addition to the marathon.

His work at Harvester was going relatively well, and often during his long highway runs, he reflected on his future with the company. He came to the conclusion that it would be better to quit the job just before leaving for Amsterdam.

He also found the time to teach a lively Sunday-school class in the local United church. To the 12- to 15-year-olds, his tales of working in the coal mine at age 11 sounded like fiction.

On June 23, at the provincial Olympic trials, Johnny won the Ontario 10,000-metre title in Toronto's Varsity Stadium. His exceedingly fast time of 33:46 bode well for the upcoming national trials. Snell placed second.

The 1928 Olympic trials were creating considerable excitement, not only in Hamilton but across the entire country. For the first time, the Canadian government announced that it was allocating $26,000 towards team expenses in Amsterdam. Other years, the various sports federations had had to shoulder the full financial responsibility, in co-operation with the Canadian Olympic committee. It was also suggested that any athlete who established a new Canadian record at the Hamilton trials would have some of his or her expenses covered by the Olympic committee.

Because he now lived in the province, Johnny participated as a member of the Ontario team. Nova Scotia was represented by Leigh Miller, who later moved to Hamilton, and George Irwin, of Dartmouth. Miller was entered in the 100-metre dash and ran head to head against a relatively unknown high-school student from Vancouver named Percy Williams. Irwin, 1927 Herald and Mail 10-Mile Modified Marathon winner, was one of Johnny's challengers in the 10,000-metre event.

The 10,000-metre race was billed as a Miles-versus-Snell duel, and the spectators were not disappointed. For a large portion of the race, Johnny allowed Mitchell, of the Monarch Athletic Club in Toronto, to set the pace. At the second lap, Johnny forged into the lead, finishing the distance with his trademark burst of speed. His time of 33:49.4 was a new Canadian record. This time, Snell placed third.

In the trial competitions on Saturday, June 30, Percy Williams won the 100-metre event, tying the Olympic record and establishing a new Canadian time of 10.6 seconds. He also won the 200-metre event, signalling that he was a runner to be reckoned with in Amsterdam.

A marathon was not scheduled because trials for that event had taken place the previous year. Cliff Bricker, who had established a new Canadian marathon record by winning it, was already training on a farm outside Amsterdam.

Six new Canadian records were established during the trials, and 25 track and field athletes were selected for the men's Olympic team. Cyril Coaffee, of Winnipeg's North End Club, 1927 sprint champion and member of the 1920 and 1924 Canadian Olympic track teams, was outdistanced in all heats, denying him the opportunity to make it to three Olympics in a row.

Shortly before the departure for Amsterdam, and thanks to a second $5,000 donation from the Ontario government and donations from the Nova Scotia and Prince Edward Island governments, two athletes were added to the track and field team. One of them was Nova Scotian Silas McLellan.

McLellan, once called the "silent farmer from Hants County," discovered road racing after he returned from overseas duty in World War I. Recognizing his agility and speed, neighboring farmers would hire him each fall to round up their cattle. With his dog, McLellan would outrun the steer and rope it. In competition, he racked up marathon wins in

Halifax in 1930 and 1931, and many times he finished among the top five in the Herald and Mail 10-Mile Modified Marathon. But it was his competitive spirit that made him a Maritime hero. Rarely did he not finish a race, and it was said he often travelled to Halifax to run a long-distance race in the morning before returning to his Noel, Hants County, farm to do a full afternoon's work and head out for an evening of dancing. The long-time postmaster would run his last race at age 48.

At a banquet sponsored by the City of Hamilton at the Royal Connaught Hotel, Mayor William Burton congratulated the athletes for their tremendous effort, adding that he took pride in the work of the organizers and in the enthusiastic community support.

One week later, on July 11, Johnny boarded the SS *Albertic* in Montreal, joining track and field team members for a voyage to Amsterdam, via London. They stopped briefly in Quebec City, where they were welcomed by civic officials and were taken on a brief sightseeing tour. Soon, they were back on board and heading down the St. Lawrence River, out into the Atlantic.

8 Amsterdam Olympics, 1928

For security reasons, the Canadian Olympic committee had decided against sending the entire team on one ship. Other concerns were the lack of training facilities on board and the problem of scheduling the use of the small gymnasium and swimming pool. So, while the track and field athletes, wrestlers, and a few others travelled on the SS *Albertic,* the lacrosse team, swimmers, officials and other team members were accommodated on board the SS *Empress of Scotland,* which left a week later.

It was an exciting time for Johnny, and his first international trip without his parents. He was retracing the route he had travelled 22 years earlier as an infant moving to Canada with his family. A social neophyte, he spent much of his time on board exercising in the gymnasium and running laps around the deck. Sea voyages are notorious for increasing appetite, and Johnny had to make a special effort to stay trim for the Olympics.

When the athletes disembarked in Southampton, England, Johnny felt fine, but others complained of sore muscles. Percy Williams had sore ankles from running on the hard deck of the ship, and one of the wrestlers suffered infected burns on various parts of his body—the result of training on soiled mats.

Marathoner Cliff Bricker, in top form after three months of intensive training in the Dutch province of Groningen, was on hand to greet his track and field teammates when they arrived in Amsterdam. His Olympic-trial time of 2:44.24.4 was a new Canadian record, though considerably slower than Johnny's 1926 Boston record-breaking finish. In recognition of Bill Reynolds' recent successes, an attempt was made to have him replace Silas McLellan in the marathon event.

On the Sunday prior to the July 28 opening of the Games, Bricker took the other members of the marathon contingent on a tour of the Olympic stadium and the marathon route. For six hours, they studied every detail and were unimpressed with the course, with the condition of the roads, and with the lack of hot water at the stadium.

The day before the official opening, the French team tried to enter the stadium but was refused admission. After receiving an apology—and then being harassed a second time by the same gatekeeper—team members decided to boycott the opening ceremonies. They even threatened to withdraw from the Games but were talked out of it.

The Canadian team, booked into the Holland Hotel, had been taken under the wing of a hospitality committee set up by 10 Dutch businesses. The citizens of Amsterdam were also displaying a lot of interest in the Canadians. "The Canadians and Americans are the centre of interest on the streets," said the *Winnipeg Evening Tribune.* "They are inevitably followed by curious crowds and many Europeans spend considerable time about the hotel which houses the Canucks."

The Americans were attracting interest of another kind, too. U.S. athletes were complaining about their accommodations aboard a ship chartered for that purpose, the SS *Roosevelt,* and they complained about the distance between the ship and the Olympic stadium. Another sore point was the ratio of coaches to athletes. Some of the runners, including Clarence DeMar, were upset because several "coaches" appeared to be along just for the ride.

On opening day, more than 40,000 spectators filled the stadium, while a disappointed spill-over crowd—estimated at 75,000—stood outside. Forty-three nations were represented by 4,000 athletes. Security at the stadium was so tight that many participants found themselves on the outside without their proper identification pass and unable to get back in. The Finnish athletes had to scale the stadium fence in order to get past the opening-day crowd.

With Prince Hendrik of Holland looking on, the cannon boomed, the Olympic flag was raised, and a thousand pigeons were released. In the centre of the stadium, Johnny stood proudly among his fellow Canadians and wiped tears from his eyes. The Canadian team made quite an impression in their smart white-and-red parade uniforms. The women wore skirts and jackets that they had brought with them from Canada; but many of the men wore uniforms tailored hastily in Amsterdam after it was decided that their Canadian-made outfits were too shabby from the ocean crossing.

During competition, Canada was a major surprise. Percy Williams' performance was the highlight of the men's track and field competition: Not only did he shut out the top U.S. sprinters—McAllister, "the flying cop," and Frank Wykoff, of the Los Angeles Athletic Club—he also beat Jack London, a great runner from British Guiana, and Germany's George Lammers, who finished second and third behind Williams in the 100-metre event. The stadium crowd went wild, but nobody expected Williams to repeat the feat in the 200-metre. Previously, no Canadian had won even one of these two sprints in Olympic competition, and only two competitors, Americans Archie Hahn (1904) and Bill Craig (1912), had won the two events during the same Games.

When Williams won the qualifying round and the 200-metre semifinal, the crowd was abuzz. Few knew that this newcomer from British Columbia had worked his way across Canada as a railroad dining-car waiter in order to attend the national trials in Hamilton. Labelled alternately as 19 or 20 years old, Williams was portrayed in the press as untrained and overly ambitious. He was, in fact, a fine-tuned sprinter coached by the unorthodox Bob Granger. He was running with a heart damaged by a childhood bout of rheumatic fever.

In the stretch of the final heat in the 200-metre competition, Williams flashed in front and won the event narrowly over Rangeley, of Britain. Jackson Scholz, of the United States, and Helmut Koernig, of Germany, tied for third. Charlie Paddock, the California star whose amateur status had been challenged so often, said of Williams after being ousted in the semifinal, "He doesn't run—he flies."

Although the distances were different, Williams' winning strategy was not unlike that which Johnny used. Both preferred to trail the front runner for the first part of the race and then, at an opportune time, push into the lead and finish the contest in a great burst of speed.

Amsterdam was the first Olympiad to include women's track and field events, and Canada won two of the five competitions. In the high jump, Ethel Catherwood, originally from Ontario, caught the imagination of the press and public with a winning performance of five feet, 2.5 inches. The Canadian women's 400-metre relay team brought the surprised spectators to their feet with a sparkling victory. Relay-team member Myrtle Cook might well have won the 100-metre competition, because she had set a world's record in the event a few months earlier, but was disqualified in the final after two false starts.

The number of entries for the 10,000-metre run was quite large, so Canadian officials decided to scratch their competitors in that event and save them for the marathon. That decision came as a blow to Johnny, who had been looking forward to challenging the world's top two middle-distance runners—Finns Paavo Nurmi and Willie Ritola. While Nurmi had run the distance more than three-and-a-half minutes faster than Johnny's Canadian record time, Johnny felt the experience would have been a good primer for the marathon.

Seventy-five runners representing 24 countries jostled at the starting line for the marathon, all of them aware of the rules governing the event. Dutch officials had compiled a list warning that a runner could be disqualified for: not wearing a clean uniform, jumping into the canal to cool off, taking refreshments from unofficial refreshment stations, taking rides, or interfering with other runners.

As they left the stadium on the circuitous route along the canals and out into the countryside, Johnny was well in back of the front runners. The weather was damp and cool, and Johnny was hoping to place among the leaders. But almost immediately, he was plagued by bits of sand and small stones that made their way into his running shoes. He wanted to stop and shake them out but was afraid that he would lose momentum. At the halfway mark, Johnny noticed that many of the competitors had dropped out, mostly with sore feet from the hard, level highway. The course was slightly monotonous, with no hills and dips to break up the grind. The remaining runners were stretched out in a long, straggly line, with American Joie Ray well out in front in a battle with Martti Marttelin, of Finland, and Yamada Kanematsu, of Japan.

Nearing the stadium, Johnny's pace began to falter as the blisters on his feet began to break and bleed through his thick socks. Envisioning the 1927 Boston Marathon that he had not finished, he was determined to finish at all costs, even though he knew he could not win. Just outside of the stadium, he could hear the roar of the crowd as it rose to see the first runner. Spectators expected to see one of the Finns or an American but were shocked to see a frail, exhausted figure wearing the colors of France.

At approximately the 20-mile point, El Abdul Baghinel Ouafi, an Algerian-born automobile worker from Paris, had appeared out of no-where and held the lead to the end, breaking the tape in 2:32.57. Twenty-six seconds later, another relative unknown, Chilean newsboy Miquel Plaza, crossed the finish line to applause and wild cheering. The three runners from Finland, Japan, and the United States, who had held the lead earlier, followed Plaza to take third, fourth, and fifth places. El Ouafi's time was 19 minutes faster than that of Bill Sherring, the only Canadian ever to win an Olympic marathon.

Johnny made his last lap around the Olympic stadium to claim 16th place in a time of 2:43.32. It had taken every ounce of Cape Breton grit to stay in the race. Cliff Bricker had also suffered from blistered feet but managed to finish 10th. Silas McLellan recorded a 24th-place finish. For the United States, Michelson was ninth, and DeMar had his poorest finish in his long career, crossing the line in 27th spot. Henigan placed 39th.

Unable to walk back to their hotel because of the condition of their feet, Johnny and Bricker were driven in an ambulance.

Sixty years later, Johnny clings to the belief that his father's presence in Amsterdam would have provided the impetus that he seemed to be lacking. He could see the positive influence that Percy Williams' coach had had on the sprinter's performance. There were many distractions in the Dutch city, and it is possible that Mr. Miles may have inspired his son to develop a clearer strategy to meet the demands of the flat marathon course. Mr. Miles had wanted to attend but could not afford it.

Nevertheless, Johnny joined the rest of the Canadian contingent in taking comfort in the team's overall showing. The U.S. track and field team, on the other hand, was discouraged. Members had been outclassed in 14 of the 22 men's events and in four of the five women's events. There had been much criticism of their behavior on the SS *Roosevelt* and at the Games. The press called them "over-confident," "over-trained," and "over-fed."

With the 1932 Olympics tagged for Los Angeles, the Americans had time to analyse their mistakes in Amsterdam and to prepare for what was described later as "the greatest athletic show on earth."

Spirits were high on board the SS *Albertic* during the return voyage. Free from their training routine, Johnny and his colleagues enjoyed the luxury and comfort of the ocean liner. An easy conversationalist, Johnny realized, nevertheless, that shipboard socializing required more: On more than one occasion, his inability to dance left him isolated. He had no desire to smoke, and the behavior of some of the athletes under the influence of alcohol confirmed his hesitancy about the habit. But dancing was something else. Johnny met many attractive women during the trip and soon appreciated the disadvantage of being a non-dancer. He resolved to learn the skill.

For the remainder of the voyage, he amused himself by reading, playing some of the shipboard games, and watching the waves and the occasional iceberg float by. He was looking forward to arriving home.

*Johnny addresses
Amherst well-wishers.*

*Boston Caledonia Games,
1926. Left to right:
Jimmie Henigan, Whitey
Michelson, Johnny, games
president Walter Scott,
Clarence DeMar,
Karl Koski.*

*Running with
Lillian in
Boston, 1926.*

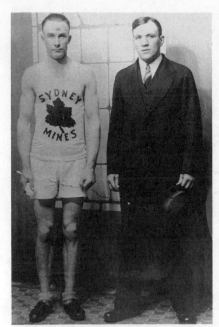

Billy Taylor (left) and trainer
Jack McKenna.

Roy Oliver.

Johnny runs against Clarence DeMar
(wearing the gloves) in Glace Bay, 1927.
Johnny won, and John Miles Williston
was named.

Johnny, number 20, poses with
Hamilton Olympic Athletic
Club members.

9 The Second Crowning

Before leaving for Amsterdam, Johnny had informed the manager at the International Harvester plant that he would not be returning to his job. He had said it would be unfair to hold his position open when others were looking for work, and beyond that, Johnny had expressed a desire to take on something more challenging. Appreciating Johnny's candor, the manager had suggested that they discuss it again after the Olympics.

In early September 1928, Johnny made his way to the Hamilton general office and, after a brief interview, was offered a job as inspector, back on the second floor of the fibre and twine plant. Slightly concerned that a discussed training course had not materialized, he accepted on condition that he be given a future opportunity to learn the manufacturing and business end of the company. For now, Johnny had other priorities.

Early in the new year, he heard about a local dance studio that was offering lessons to men and women. He convinced his sister Lena to sign up with him and, before long, considered himself quite a dancer. Lena was not so sure of her brother's prowess, but she agreed to arrange a date for him and asked a friend who worked as a stenographer.

Johnny recalls that his bright-eyed date did not seem terribly impressed. "But I was really taken with her, even if she didn't really encourage me." Twenty-year-old Bess Connon was outgoing and sophisticated, perhaps a bit too much for Johnny's liking. She, on the other hand, was unnerved by this puritanical young man who had so much energy that he rarely sat still.

They saw each other occasionally after that first date, but when Bess came to the Miles house, more often than not it was to visit Lena. It was just as well: Mr. and Mrs. Miles were determined that nothing distract Johnny from winning again in Boston.

In early January, he began training in anticipation of winning several major races before the Boston Marathon. By early spring, Johnny and his father had worked out a demanding regime. Running 10 miles a day, sometimes going 20 along the Hamilton-Niagara Falls highway, Johnny was feeling in top form.

One day, not long before the 15-mile Easter weekend race in Toronto, he felt pains in the back of his legs. But with the help of rubdowns from his father and wonderful massages from John Beer at the YMCA, the knots in Johnny's legs seemed to disappear. He had to be mentally, as well as physically, fit in Boston, and a victory in Toronto would help heal his bruised ego.

Among the 46 runners at the Toronto starting line on March 29 were fellow Olympians Cliff Bricker and Billy Reynolds, but almost immediately, Johnny had the lead to himself. He was trying something different by jumping out in front, and his opponents were obviously surprised. The top challengers caught up with him, however, and only a last-minute sprint gave him the victory. Johnny reached the finish a mere 20 seconds ahead of Reynolds, for a time of 1:23.5.50 Snell ran third, and Bricker was a close fourth.

The win, Johnny's first over Bricker, boosted his confidence. He could now ride into Boston—if not on a charger, well, at least with his head held high.

A few Boston scribes were inspired to ask themselves whether Johnny had finally overcome his 1927 disappointment and humiliation. Was he now ready to do battle with the classy runners out to challenge DeMar's stranglehold on the Boston classic?

High on the list of possible spoilers was Karl Koski, always a strong finisher but never a winner. DeMar was the favorite because of his repeat victory in 1928, which gave him the enviable record of six first-place finishes in 12 attempts. But "DeMar-a-thon" said he was not up for the race and estimated that he would need two hours and 45 minutes to complete it. Koski's clubmate Villar Kyronen was also given an outside chance, while Whitey Michelson, rumored to be suffering from a gimpy knee, was not pegged as much of a threat. Of the Canadians entered, Silas McLellan was once again picked as the one to watch, because he had finished 10th the year before.

When the Mileses left for Boston on April 17, there was no big send-off and no fancy hotel paid for by supporters. The city had sent many runners to Boston since the advent of the marathon in 1897, and Johnny shared the sports spotlight that year with a stable of fine athletes. The family arranged its own accommodation with Mr. and Mrs. Murdock Williams in Dorchester, the Boston suburb that was the home of Jimmie Henigan's athletic club.

Meanwhile, Sydney Mines fans were wishing Billy Taylor luck in the same race. Considering the nature of the town in the 1920s, it was not surprising that the person who had replaced Johnny as local favorite shared a similar background. Taylor, three years older than Johnny, had emigrated from Scotland with his parents in 1910. His father found work in the mines and expected his son to follow him. But as a teenager, Taylor left Sydney Mines to sail the world as a merchant seaman. By the time he returned in 1923, Johnny was one year into his fledgling running career. Taylor soon joined his father in the coal mine, and he later got a job delivering groceries for the co-op—just as Johnny had.

It is conceivable that Taylor was among the hundreds of well-wishers who cheered Johnny to a Sydney Mines victory on September 23, 1923. Three years later, after being encouraged by friends to take up the sport, Taylor won his first road race. He had just turned 24.

Now, in 1929, he was following Johnny's path to Boston, and the proprietor of the Strand Theatre had arranged a collection for him. Mayor Dwyer wished Taylor luck and drew him aside to ask him to pass on best wishes to Johnny.

Johnny was confident but was understandably wary of the press after the lambasting he had suffered two years before. "If you win a race," he was quoted as saying in Boston, "you're a hero, but if you lose, even though you've trained faithfully and done your best, you're just a lemon. I've learned enough not to care what they say about me now." But Johnny did care, as part of a team effort with Harold Webster and Frank Hughes, of the Hamilton Olympic Athletic Club. He spent his free time before the race relaxing and trying to stay loose.

Old ties are hard to sever, and the newspapers had difficulty associating Johnny with any place in Canada other than Cape Breton. One described him as, "Johnny Miles, diminutive Twine Inspector, from Sydney Mines [who] bore the Maple Leaf for Canada."

"I think the race will be a hard one," Johnny told a sports reporter covering his pre-race activities. "Koski is good and so is DeMar. I'm [also] going to keep an eye on Billy Taylor. He can win. I'll be there. I feel fine, and you can bet I think I'm going to win. I expect a fight and am ready for it."

On race day, doctors John Connors and Arthur White gave each runner a medical checkup. Johnny was declared fit, his heart running like a clock. In high spirits, he declined to be weighed in, telling them that he was a trim 136 pounds. The weather, too, was just what the doctor ordered—warm, with a cool breeze. Johnny planned to use his proven strategy of hanging back, and this time, there was no secret weapon. He sported running shoes somewhat better than the 98-cent co-op sneakers he had made famous in 1926—and infamous in 1927. There was also no last-minute steak and toast. Number 113's only concern as he joined the 187 other competitors was the recurring muscle spasms and knots in his calf and thighs.

At the crack of the pistol, Johnny jostled his way through the mass of runners and claimed seventh position. He was content to stay there, always keeping the leaders well in view. Jack Lamb, of the Dorchester Club, was lead man, and between him and Johnny was the cream of the North American marathon world: Koski, Michelson, Kyronen, DeMar, and Taylor, in that order.

At South Framington, the crowd was amazed to see Lamb setting such a frantic pace. He continued through Natick and on to Wellesley: An upset was in the making.

At the five-mile point, Koski and Johnny had appeared to be straining and in considerable trouble. Koski looked tired, and Johnny's leg muscles were tightening up, the tendons in his heels cramping. The pain was clearly visible on his face. He bit into his cheek and began running on the tips of his toes, hoping it would relieve the tension. Remarkably, the pain subsided, and Johnny knew that he had won the first round.

Lamb eventually dropped back and finished fifth.

When Johnny noticed that DeMar was slowing and dropping back, he moved up and passed him in a spurt usually reserved for the final stretch. Michelson and Kyronen were left behind, too. Despite his reported bad knee, Michelson was running well, and at Lake Street, five miles from the finish, he caught up to Johnny. For a short distance, they ran together. Johnny wondered if this seesaw battle with DeMar and Michelson was a conspiracy to wear him out, but he quickly dismissed the idea, concentrating instead on maintaining his pace.

And then the muscle spasms returned. If not for the need to ward off Michelson, Johnny may have given in to the pain. He had lost all sense of time, and the overpowering urge to break the tape began to consume him. At one point on Wellesley Hills—the section of the course most feared by even veteran contestants—Johnny and Taylor ran neck and neck before Johnny dashed ahead.

At Coolidge Corner, Johnny decided to go for broke. With only a few miles to go, a reporter had advised him that his pace was already two minutes better than DeMar's record. Koski and Kyronen were now his main challengers. Forgetting about his sore muscles, Johnny reached again into his storehouse of energy and headed for the tape, stretched out like a beacon a few yards ahead. The feel of the tape pressing against his chest felt better than a Beer massage, and the roar of the crowd topped it all off—Johnny knew that he had done it.

His comeback before half a million spectators was made all the more sweet by the record-breaking time of 2:33.8.8—three minutes and 59 seconds faster than DeMar had run the year before. Over the next 10 years, only four runners would better that time.

Koski was two minutes and 18 seconds behind, 18 seconds ahead of Kyronen. Michelson hobbled across in fourth place, baffling the pundits who had ruled him out.

As he was savoring his victory, Johnny found himself in the arms of a smallish, grey-haired woman with moist, sparkling eyes. When his mother whispered to him in a shaky voice, "Johnny, you're the most wonderful boy in the world," a cheer rose up all around them.

Just as he caught a glimpse of his father waiting to congratulate him as well, Johnny was picked up off the ground in a great bear hug from Massachusetts governor Frank G. Allen. Throwing all protocol to the wind, the governor blurted out, "You are a wonderful boy, and it pleases me greatly to see you win after having the courage to come up all the way from Canada to run." This exchange brought another loud cheer from the crowd.

Amidst the confusion and the press of the people, Johnny asked where he could find a Western Union office. Someone pointed to one nearby, and Johnny rushed off to send a simple message: "I won dear, I'm coming back Monday." When Bess received the telegram in Hamilton at the home of her parents, Alexander and Annie Connon, she was overjoyed.

When he returned to the clubhouse, reporters teased Johnny about his girl. He explained that he was not actually engaged to Bess and had, in fact, met her only recently. "But maybe I'll have a better chance now," he said. Egged on by the reporters, he added, "She's the most wonderful girl in the world, next to my mother, that is."

One of the reporters who sought Johnny out was Bill Cunningham, of the *Boston Post*. He apologized for what he had written in 1927 and admitted that in all his years in the newspaper business, no other article had generated such a backlash. Johnny accepted Cunningham's apology and then, as if a great weight had been lifted from his shoulders, walked out of the BAA clubhouse. Any self-doubts he had had were gone forever.

Within minutes of the victory, news of the feat interrupted a children's matinee and flashed across the screen of the Strand Theatre, in Sydney Mines. A wild cheer broke out from the audience, which included many youngsters who remembered the teenager with the handkerchief wrapped around his hand. Johnny later received a congratulatory telegram from Sydney Mines mayor Mike Dwyer.

In Boston, the Mileses again received invitations to banquets and receptions, but they decided to restrict their itinerary to a few personal appearances and to a Cape Breton Club banquet in Johnny's honor. Also on the list was a visit to the Keith-Albee Theatre, where Johnny met the screen star Lita Gray.

Two days after the race—the day he had promised Bess he would return to Hamilton—Johnny and his parents visited Governor Allen in his office, where Johnny received a brief lecture on the benefits of marriage. Later, in response to an interviewer's question about rumors of a pending wedding, Johnny confirmed his commitment to bachelorhood. "Me, get married? I should say not," he said. "I'm too busy, I haven't time."

All of the Canadian runners who remained in Boston attended the Cape Breton Club banquet at the Intercolonial Club. Eighth-place finisher Ronald O'Toole, of Newfoundland, was asked to join in the festivities; and he reciprocated by inviting Johnny and Billy Taylor—who had finished a respectable sixth in 2:40.05— to the dinner the Newfoundland Club was throwing for him in another part of the building. Johnny was asked to say a few words to the Newfoundland Club banquet. In conclusion, he said, "I would rather be beaten by Ron O'Toole, who I consider to be a real sport, than any other competitor." It had been no easy task for O'Toole to make his way to Boston, where he had completed his first marathon 40 seconds ahead of Clarence DeMar, despite seriously damaged feet.

Among the articles published in newspapers throughout the United States and Canada after Johnny's comeback victory was one that appeared in the Halifax *Herald*. The paper said that the win "warmed the hearts of his own people, for despite his removal from Sydney Mines and Nova Scotia, the people of the province still claim him as their own. It was under

Nova Scotia colors that he made his sensational win in the same event in 1926 and it was as a Nova Scotia boy that he went out and repeated yesterday in glorious style."

In winning the Boston classic, Johnny became the first non-resident of the United States to be declared winner of the U.S. National Marathon Championship. Considered a thinking marathoner who nevertheless displayed an incredible ability to charge up hills and sprint to the finish, he was being touted as the distance runner of the age. He always plotted his next move and usually knew whether to continue or withdraw—sometimes not too gracefully.

10 Running Out the Clock

Hamilton city officials were no slouches 60 years ago when it came to throwing celebrations. When marathoner Jack Caffery returned from Boston victorious in 1900 and 1901, almost everyone in town turned out to greet him. By 1929, the city had grown considerably—and you had to be quite important in order to receive such a reception. To welcome home Johnny and his parents, thousands of citizens lined the streets leading to city hall, where a number of dignitaries spoke glowingly of Johnny's comeback.

While not a new experience for the runner, this was somehow different. Johnny found himself paying particular attention to the words of his boss, W.E. Worth, manager of International Harvester's fibre and twine division. "If Miles put as much time and energy into the interests of International Harvester as he puts into running," Worth said, "maybe someday he'll have a future with it."

Johnny recalls that he did not sleep very well that night. He tossed and turned trying to clarify the real message behind his boss' words. Was he criticizing Johnny for neglecting his job or for not being ambitious enough? Was he offering the long-awaited opportunity for advancement? Or was Johnny reading too much into the speech? Then he thought about his racing options, whether he should train for the 1930 British Empire Games or whether he should participate in another Olympics, this time in Los Angeles in 1932.

The next morning, Johnny approached Worth. He admitted that his education was limited but said he was willing to study at night school if the company showed it had confidence in him. The next day, he was promoted to a foreman's position, and Johnny stuck to his promise: Over the next few years, he took several night courses at Hamilton Technical School in industrial chemistry, mechanical drawing, machine-shop practices, and engineering. With training and teaching Sunday school, he had little time left to court Bess.

Johnny participated in several races in the Maritimes and in Ontario and was looking forward to making a good showing at the August 1930 British Empire Games, the first running of the games that would become the Commonwealth Games. He also decided to return to Boston to defend his record, believing that he could still improve on it and maybe even surpass DeMar's string of six victories. Johnny was obviously not ready to retire. He had acquired an assortment of running shoes, and they were not worn out yet.

On June 1, 1929, Billy Taylor gave Johnny something to think about when deciding his future. Johnny had received an invitation to return to Glace Bay, Cape Breton, to participate in an exhibition 10-mile event on the Black Diamond Race Track. Fred Ward, New York long-distance ace and holder of the Canadian marathon title, was on the card, together with two Cape Breton challengers: Danny MacDonald, from Baddeck, and New Waterford's Johnny McLeod.

Reporters were working overtime to hype the race as a real thriller. Johnny and Ward had better credentials, but local runners Taylor, MacDonald, and McLeod were picked to finish on top, in that order. MacDonald had surprised everyone by outdistancing Taylor in the 1928 inaugural Sydney-to-Glace Bay 13-mile run. His 39th-place finish that same year in Boston made him someone to watch.

The invitational race fell on one of the hottest days of the year. From the start, Taylor was in the lead, while a listless Johnny found himself in fifth spot. Ward was doing much better but was biding his time, and MacDonald and McLeod were holding their own. No one was really challenging Taylor. By the seventh mile and to Johnny's chagrin, Taylor had lapped him, something few runners had ever done. The response of the overflow crowd was deafening, and Taylor was spurred on to sprint to the tape for a time of 55:10. He had finished a full lap ahead of the whole field.

Ward, MacDonald, McLeod, and Johnny finished in that order, and the fifth-place runner, always a favorite, received a warm ovation. People speculated that Taylor might have established a world record if he had been more strongly challenged by Ward or Johnny, and it was widely accepted that Taylor's time that day would probably never be surpassed on the cinder track. He was as fresh at the finish line as he had been at the start.

Thus followed a series of ups and downs in Johnny's running career. On September 21, he won the Hamilton Marathon sponsored by his sports alma mater, the Hamilton Olympic Athletic Club. His time was 2:46.25.

The following April, the Mileses made their fourth visit to Boston for the marathon. The odds-on favorite, Johnny had little to prove after a spectacular first-try victory and a gritty second win.He acted more like a tourist rather than a runner in quest of success, and later, some suggested that the champion had been lacking in spirit.

Another runner who caught the imagination of the forecasters that year was Karl Koski, who had won the U.S. National Marathon, March 22 in New York, in a time of 2:35.21. DeMar, also not ready to retire, had more than his share of loyal supporters, and he was picked to finish among the first five. At 41, the greying DeMar was always considered a threat. Whitey Michelson was back for another try, as was Jimmie Henigan, who had missed the 1929 race. Much attention was being paid to Newfoundlander Ronald O'Toole, who had come to Boston more than a week in advance and was expressing the same spirit of confidence that Johnny had first displayed in 1926. Reports of O'Toole's vigorous training schedule, under coach Ned Payne, caught the imagination of the press and of race officials. On race day, he was an even bet to place at least third, after Johnny and Koski. Nova Scotians Billy Taylor, Silas McLellan, Alf Rodgers, and Johnny McLeod were all back and were expected to run well.

April 19 was a wet, sultry day. It rained through most of the race—hardly ideal conditions for any of the 180 competitors. DeMar preferred hot weather, while Johnny was at his best on cool, clear days. Number 25 doubted from the start whether he would break any records that day. It was the kind of weather that usually produced the unexpected, and that is exactly what the hundreds of thousands of spectators got.

Hans Oldag, of Buffalo, New York, emerged from the first group to fight his way to the front of the pack and, for the next 14 miles, set a relatively slow Boston pace. DeMar stayed with him for most of the distance, followed by the Finnish runners, Kyronen and Koski. Then came O'Toole and Johnny. Grouped together around Wellesley Hills, the front runners noticed that DeMar had pulled within talking distance of Oldag. As he passed the Buffalo runner, DeMar shouted over his shoulder, "Who are you, anyway?" Not waiting for a reply, he sped away on his favorite stretch of the course, never looking back and quickly widening the distance between himself and the rest of the competition. Oldag eventually finished in 57th, and DeMar went on to his seventh Boston victory in 20 years of entering the race. His time of 2:34.38 was almost two minutes slower than Johnny's 1929 record pace.

Kyronen held on to second place, with Koski a close third. Two Canadians—Gabriel Ruotsalainen, from Montreal, and Webster, of Hamilton—registered strong finishes to claim fourth and fifth positions. O'Toole, showing real grit, took sixth overall by limping across the finish line in his stocking feet. Both Henigan and McLellan finally beat Johnny: Henigan placed eighth, and McLellan was ninth. Johnny received an enthusiastic reception as he and Bill Kennedy, winner of the 1917 race, crossed the finish line hand in hand. Officially, Johnny was given 11th place, while Kennedy was accorded 12th.

Johnny was in surprisingly high spirits and acknowledged that he had not had the drive to challenge; but his unexpected showing prompted sportswriters and fans to speculate on his future. The *Herald*'s Ahern, one of Johnny's most loyal supporters, chastised him for his lacklustre effort. "The great Miles, backed by thousands of former Maritime residents and just as many natives of Boston, was a great disappointment," Ahern wrote. "He didn't show anything that looked like winning ability at any stage in the race and he was laboring after the eighth mile, apparently content to take matters easy when he found the sultry weather had an effect on his condition. It was all Miles before the race and there were very few betters who cared to wager against him."

Back in Hamilton, Bess waited anxiously for a telegram. When none arrived, she knew that the Marathon King had been dethroned. "Maybe now," she thought, "Johnny will have more time to spend with me."

Over the next few years, Johnny would run in a number of races in Hamilton and in Nova Scotia, but in only one of three major competitions—the British Empire Games—would he show an inkling of his old spirit and determination.

Preparations for the games had been going on for several years. One of the prime movers behind the project was *Hamilton Spectator* sports editor Bobby Robinson, who had helped Johnny find a job in 1927. He was also a leading figure in Canada's Olympic organization. Robinson and the national organizing committee for the Empire games, headed by E.W. Beatty, faced numerous difficulties before opening day. A few members of the British Olympic committee tried to scuttle the games by suggesting to other national Olympic organizations that fund raising for the Empire games would detract from their campaigns to send athletes to the 1932 Olympics. It was also suggested that the Empire games were a ploy by some countries to highlight their criticism of the Olympics as being unfair to smaller nations. Robinson launched a scheme to provide subsidies for teams travelling long distances; and there were rumors that he had twisted the arm of influential English sports patron Lord Darby, not only to ensure that the British participated in Hamilton but also that they contributed money to the travel fund. From that point onward, preparations went fairly smoothly.

Hamilton taxpayers footed the bill for a $110,000 indoor swimming pool and a $33,000 expansion to the stadium so that it could seat 15,000. The city also undertook to house and feed all contestants—the Australian and New Zealand contingents, for instance, were to be in town for five weeks. The Prince of Wales School was selected as suitable for billeting all athletes except the women swimmers, who were put up in the Royal Connaught Hotel. A dining room was erected on the school ground. It was estimated that the operation of the games would cost $60,000.

All games facilities were within walking distance of the civic stadium, and living just across the street, Johnny and his family were in the thick of things. During the training period leading up to the games, the Mileses' Balsam Avenue house was a regular meeting place for many well-known Canadian athletes, including star sprinter Percy Williams.

This time, Williams did not need to work his way to Hamilton. Upon his return from Amsterdam in 1928, appreciative Vancouver fans had given him a sports car. He was being billed as "the world's fastest human" and was favored to take both the 100-yard and 200-yard events.

On the eve of the games, which lasted from August 16 to 23, the press reported, "Hamilton tonight donned its holiday dress as it awaited the opening of the British Empire Games. Crowds on the street tonight gave voice to speculation on the results, particularly of tomorrow's events, when the track and field performers will make their debut."

The marathon was expected to be a race to the wire between H.W. Payne, England's record holder, and Duncan McLeod Wright, Scotland's distance champion. Fans were shocked to hear that Payne was struck by an automobile while on a training jog and was a doubtful starter. Newfoundland's Ronald O'Toole was being touted, at least by his team-mates, as having a chance of winning. Johnny was the favorite of many

Hamiltonians—and of a few Nova Scotians—but his name did not figure prominently in the betting.

A crowd in excess of 17,000 watched as Newfoundland, then the oldest British dominion, led the parade of athletes in a colorful opening-day procession, the likes of which had never been seen in Canada. Percy Williams later took the amateur's oath on behalf of the 450 athletes and officials from 11 countries.

Over the course of the week, the 50-odd competitions—ranging from lawn bowling to weight lifting—attracted thousands of spectators. Williams was a crowd pleaser, pulling a muscle on his final run in the 100-yard dash but managing to win anyway, in 9.9 seconds.

The marathon turned out to be an unforgettable contest resulting in a victory and new course record for Scotland's Wright, in 2:43.13. Sam Ferris, of England, was second, and the standardbearer for Canada was Johnny, who placed a strong third—one of his best efforts in some time. O'Toole came in eighth.

By all accounts, the Empire games were an outstanding success. The *Manitoba Free Press* reported that business in Hamilton was to be suspended on day five of the games so residents could attend. A closing-day crowd of 18,000 celebrated Canadian victories in 19 events, including six track and field contests.

Encouraged by his showing in the Empire games, Johnny decided to make a last attempt at winning again in Boston. He spent the winter working, attending night school, courting Bess, and training regularly.

That spring, Mr. and Mrs. Miles paid their last visit to the city that had become so important to them since Johnny had won there five years before. Patriot's Day, 1931, was almost as hot as it had been in 1927, when melting asphalt found its way into Johnny's super-thin sneakers. Almost from the outset, Johnny did not feel confident. The night before, he had been in high spirits, convinced that he would better his 11th-place finish of the previous year. But Johnny did not run well in hot weather. The only comfort he could take in the stifling conditions was the knowledge that few records would be set on such a day.

The heat began to affect results immediately, as runner after runner dropped out from exhaustion. Only the hardy—and foolhardy—stayed with it. At Newton hills, more competitors collapsed on the sidelines.

Only one Canadian, Dave Komonen, of Sudbury, Ontario, was among the front runners, which included Frank Cerny, of Pittsburg, David Fagerlund, of the NY Finnish Club, Clarence DeMar, New Yorker

Fred Ward, and Jimmie Henigan. These select few were soon joined by Karl Koski, while Johnny held back, always keeping the front runners within view.

The first 10 runners maintained a steady pace, but there was no flashy finish. Henigan, who had moved into the lead, was never seriously challenged. Despite a slow finishing time of 2:46.04—the poorest first-place time since J.J. McDermott's 1897 win—Henigan was understandably ecstatic: He had finally won the Boston classic after entering 11 times and completing the course only three times. To do it, he had had to overcome an agonizing, large blister that developed at the 22-mile point when one of his cotton socks twisted around in his running shoe. He contemplated dropping out, slowing his pace almost to a walk, but he continued, and fortunately, he had a four-minute lead on his competitors.

Ward was second, and Koski finished third. DeMar's fifth place was only 21 seconds ahead of Wyer, and Komonen, who ran shoulder to shoulder with Henigan for about six miles, took seventh. Three years later, the miner from Sudbury would join the list of Canadians to win in Boston.

Johnny finished 10th, one better than in 1930, but his time of 3:4.56 was one of the slowest of his career. Still, it was noted in eastern-Canadian newspapers that he had been the "first Nova Scotian" to finish.

Johnny's 1929 Boston Marathon record of 2:33.08 would be broken in 1933 by Leslie Pawson, a mill weaver from Pawtucket, Rhode Island. A Canadian would not top the time until 1974, when Jerome Drayton bettered it in a third-place effort.

Billy Taylor was not in Boston in 1931. Throughout the past year, he had continued to beat local runners, winning the May 24, 1930, three-mile event in Sydney for the fourth time. As Johnny had done, he became the owner of a Nathansan cup. Later, Taylor and Johnny met in Sydney Mines for the 10-mile Dominion Day race. It was their first head-to-head contest in Johnny's old home town, and both reputations were at stake. Taylor made up for his earlier disappointment, leaving Johnny behind in third place.

In November 1930, Taylor moved to Montreal to find better training opportunities. He found a job as a milkman and joined the Campbell Park Athletic Club, confident he could better his 1929 sixth-place finish in Boston. By the time of his last race, in June 1931, he was more optimistic than ever.

Sunday, June 14, was a hot, humid day, but that did not seem to bother the large crowd of Montrealers who lined the streets to watch the annual

10-mile race. Taylor was a late arrival at the Campbell Park clubhouse, the starting point of the event. During the pre-race medical examination, Dr. A.A. Lefebvre told Taylor that his heart was acting strangely. The runner passed it off as stress from rushing to the race, and although he was concerned, Lefebvre did not try to stop Taylor from running.

At the sound of the starter's pistol, the 29-year-old former miner got off to a strong start and maintained a steady pace throughout the north and west ends of the city. There was little automobile traffic, and soon the stress passed. Perhaps he knew of the doctor's warning that Clarence DeMar had received in 1911 not to enter the Boston Marathon. DeMar ran the race anyway and won.

The heat was forcing several of the 33 competitors out of the race. At approximately the eight-mile point, Taylor felt a sharp pain in his chest and collapsed, just opposite 4579 St. Andre Street. Two runners passed him before one of the contestants stopped and checked Taylor's pulse. He called officials from the sidelines and continued; Taylor was rushed to Notre Dame Hospital, where he was treated for complications from sunstroke. His condition was critical.

After Gabriel Ruotsalainen, an outstanding long-distance runner who also wore the colors of the Campbell Park Club, won the race in 1:50, he was informed that his fellow club member was on his way to hospital.

At 9:40 p.m., the inspiring career of the smooth-running marathoner from Sydney Mines came to an untimely end: Taylor died. A police investigation later absolved race organizers of any blame in the runner's death.

When news of Taylor's death filtered back to Sydney Mines, the community was shocked. If he had died in the coal mine, where he had toiled under dangerous conditions, it may have been easier to accept. Few families in the Cape Breton mining community had not experienced such grief. But to die while running in a road race was practically unthinkable.

Resisting the temptation to return to Boston in 1932, Johnny opted to prepare for the Los Angeles Olympics. He became a member of the "Depression year team," along with athletes such as Cliff Bricker, who won the 10,000-metre event at the 1932 Olympic time trials in Hamilton. Bricker was considered Canada's best hope in the gruelling marathon event. Johnny remained in great shape and was confident, but other priorities were emerging in his life.

Opening day of the Games of the 8th Olympiad, on Saturday, July 30, ushered in two weeks of warm, wonderful weather that inspired one writer

to sum up the Games as, "record weather, record crowds, record performances and record receipts." As Johnny mingled with the thousands of other
athletes in the centre of the stadium, he marvelled at the size of the
crowd—more than 105,000 people. The colorful flags and bunting—
including the new five-circle Olympic flag—the soaring pigeons, and the
marching bands made quite an impression.

The hosting committee wanted everything to be bigger and better
than ever before. For the first time in the history of the Games, there was
an Olympic Village, built especially in the Baldwin Hills district. Women
were banned from the village, however, so female athletes were housed in
the Chapman Park Hotel on Wilshire Boulevard. To assure accuracy in all
foot-race events, an automatic camera was installed at the finish line.

Boasting the largest contingent of athletes (500), the United States
would dominate in competition, winning 41 gold medals. Italy would
place second with 12 gold medals. Duncan McNaughton, a Vancouver
native and student at the University of Southern California who was added
to the team at the last minute, won the high-jump contest—Canada's only
track and field gold.

Among the stars to emerge in Los Angeles was American Babe
Didrikson, gold-medal winner in the javelin and hurdles competitions.
She probably could have won a medal in the shot-put, but women athletes
were allowed to enter only three events. In Didrikson's third, the high
jump, she won a silver medal.

Canada's great hope, Percy Williams, lost in the semifinal of the 100-
metre sprint. Although his time of 10.8 matched his record-breaking
performance in Amsterdam four years earlier, it was not even enough this
time to qualify for the finals.

A 1928 record was also shattered in the marathon, when Argentina's
Juan Carlos Zabala completed the course one minute and 21 seconds faster
than France's El Ouafi had. Canada's Cliff Bricker ran second for the first
10 miles but fell back and finished 12th. Johnny improved on his previous
16th-place Olympic finish by coming in 14th. This time, he did not
speculate that his father's presence would have made a difference. The L.A.
Olympics were Johnny's last big international marathon fling.

He returned to Hamilton and continued to take part in races there. "It
was really time to settle down to working on my career at Harvester,"
Johnny says, "and Bess was the guiding hand which could help me
succeed." After more than five years of courtship, Johnny and Bess married
on August 24, 1935, in a ceremony attended by family and a few friends

at the First United Church in Hamilton. They drove to Barrie, Ontario, for a brief honeymoon and settled into an apartment.

He considered training for the 1936 Berlin Olympic trials. Bess knew that Johnny would make up his own mind on the matter—with a little help from his father. When asked what Johnny should do, Mr. Miles told his son that he had to make his own decision.

Johnny weighed the sacrifices that accompany training and competition and opted to devote himself to Bess and to his new life. He hung up his marathon shoes in exchange for ski boots and golf shoes. Physical fitness still interests him—the legacy of his father, who always stressed the benefits of a healthy body and a clear mind.

Mr. and Mrs. Miles wish their son good luck.

Johnny, Willie Kyronen, and Karl Koski (right) receive medals from Massachusetts governor Frank G. Allen (left).

Boston Post *cartoon, 1929.*

Johnny wins bronze medal for Canada at 1930 British Empire Games.

11 International Assignments

Johnny was one of the lucky ones who continued to work throughout the Depression. Many others in the Hamilton area had to settle for intermittent, low-paid work harvesting fruit and tobacco. By 1933, Johnny had completed his on-the-job-training program and was promoted to a position of foreman.

Away from work, Johnny joined the Masonic Lodge—becoming its master in 1942—continued to teach Sunday school, and volunteered as a gymnastics instructor. When World War II broke out in 1939, Johnny was 33 years old and considered too old to serve in the armed forces. "I did my wartime service at International Harvester, where we manufactured Bren gun carriers for North Africa," he says proudly.

When the war ended, so did the life of his mother. Although not bedridden, she had been ill for some time but never revealed the nature of her illness to Johnny. He recalls that the family gathered at the Balsam Avenue house that evening in July 1945 to celebrate the discharge of Johnny's brother-in-law from the army. Johnny and Bess returned home, and as they were entering the front door, the phone was ringing. "We certainly were not prepared for the news which Lena had for us," he says. "She was quite emotional and simply told us that Mom had collapsed a few minutes after we left and had died almost immediately. Despite her age and her ill health, I was very upset; and Bess and I returned to Balsam Avenue so we could be together with other family members."

Later, Johnny and Bess moved in with Mr. Miles, who had retired, but they enjoyed only one year together before Johnny and Bess moved again.

In mid-November 1946, International Harvester advised Johnny that a posting to France was confirmed. The company—an international farm-machinery giant that had begun in 1831 when Cyrus McCormick patented a horse-drawn reaper that revolutionized farming—intended to play a role in re-establishing Europe's agricultural economy. Harvester wanted Johnny to act as assistant superintendent at its Croix Twine Mill, in Lille, France.

Johnny saw the offer as an expression of the firm's confidence in him, and he was anxious to do a good job. But Bess was reluctant to leave Canada, and the couple grappled with the problem for a long time. Recognizing that this was an opportunity that Johnny could not find in Hamilton and encouraged by family and friends, they decided to go.

The pair left for New York City early in the new year, the car jammed with belongings. Larger items had been put in storage, and Johnny's oldest sister, Lena, and her husband had agreed to care for the aging Mr. Miles. Johnny and Bess had booked sea passage across the Atlantic and were taking their car with them.

Almost from the outset, the journey was a disaster. Just outside Rochester, New York, a snowstorm reduced visibility to almost zero, and a state trooper stopped them to warn that roads ahead were impassable. Johnny and Bess found a motel, and they were forced to stay there for two days until the storm ended.

Fortunately, because their original plan had allowed for a few days in New York City, their ship was still in port when they arrived. Overwrought after the long, stressful drive, they decided to go directly to the pier.

There seemed to be a lot of confusion around the dock. Johnny stopped a policeman and asked him to point them in the direction of their ship, the *Maid Marion*. Replied the policeman in a thick Irish accent, "It's right down there, lad, just follow the road."

"You mean the one next to where the smoke is bellowing from the stack?" asked Bess.

"No, sweetheart," he said with a chuckle, "the one that's making the smoke."

Johnny asked if the ship was on fire, and the policeman said it was, though he did not know how badly it was burning. He directed the Mileses to the steamship company's office, where Johnny urged Bess to wait in the car. "Now, John," she said, "you know that you'll need me to straighten this out."

Inside the office, two young shipping clerks were trying to answer questions from hundreds of excited passengers. One of the calmer clerks explained that the ship had sustained some damage from an electrical fire and added that it would obviously not be sailing on schedule. Relieved that the fire had happened before the ship left port, the Mileses inquired about alternative arrangements and were told that another ship was leaving soon but was crowded and could not accommodate cars. Johnny and Bess opted to send their car by sea while they travelled by airplane.

In 1947, there was no jet service, and the transatlantic flight was an overnight one, though relatively comfortable and safe. The aircraft made a stopover in Iceland, where the couple spent a chilly night.

In Paris, accommodations were much better, and they stayed in a hotel for more than a week waiting for their car to arrive. They toured the city, shopped, and met with International Harvester officials to discuss Johnny's new responsibilities. Language was not a problem, because several of the officials were American and the French management people spoke English, but later, Johnny realized that a basic understanding of French was going to be necessary in order to communicate directly with employees.

When their car arrived—their furniture soaked from standing out on the dock for a week because of a strike—Johnny, Bess, and a knowledgeable guide drove to Lille. It was an even greater challenge than either of them had imagined.

Paris had been damaged during the war but not nearly so badly as the countryside had. Two years after the war's end, housing was still a problem, and Lille was no exception. Johnny and Bess stayed in a local hotel for three or four months until they found a suitable house to rent.

In the meantime, Johnny began his job and, after meeting the management personnel and supervisory staff, soon had a smooth-working management team in place. He took great pains to become better acquainted with his colleagues, and Bess was a tremendous boost to the process. Her effervescent personality was a key factor in overcoming the initial hesitancy of the local people to trust them as friends. The Mileses were outsiders, and the French were curious that a Canadian was in charge of an American company. But it was not long before most of the barriers gave way to a real sense of friendship and understanding.

Bess was lonely and homesick but overcame it by taking on the role of project manager in the remodelling of their home. The house, once occupied by a German army officer, had to be completely renovated—from plumbing to plastering. After the work was completed, the Mileses spent many pleasant evenings entertaining friends and associates in their new surroundings.

Arrangements were also made for a teacher to come to their home twice a week to tutor "Jean et Elizabeth" in the French language. On the first anniversary of their arrival in Lille, Johnny, in his best Cape Breton French accent, proposed a toast to Bess and to all of their new friends. Everyone was impressed, and Bess reciprocated with a toast to Johnny and to his promotion to plant manager. Her husband was so moved that he actually took a sip of his very first glass of wine.

In some respects, Johnny was a workaholic, yet he and Bess did find the time to take an annual vacation. For the most part, they travelled in Belgium, Denmark, Sweden, and Norway, also visiting Holland and Switzerland. In 1950, they were able to return to Canada for a three-month business trip and holiday.

The pair saw more of Europe in the autumn of 1947, when Johnny's father came to visit for five weeks. The three of them planned to motor through France, Belgium, and Britain but first made a stop, at Mr. Miles' request, at Vimy Ridge. The veteran wanted to return to the scene of the famous World War I battle in which he had fought with the Nova Scotia Highlanders on Easter Monday, 1917.

"We started out from our home in Lille in the early morning and soon arrived in the area around Douai Plain, where many a hard battle was fought," Johnny remembers. "We parked our car and walked down a lane which was draped with Canadian maple trees on both sides. We could see the twin pillars of the Vimy Ridge memorial standing on Hill 145, above Douai Plain.... Chiselled on these columns are the names of over 11,000 Canadians listed as missing or killed in action during that campaign." He said his father appreciated the opportunity to come back to Vimy, though it was a sad experience for him.

In England and Wales, the Mileses visited many relatives, most of whom Johnny and Bess had never met. They met Bess' side of the family in Scotland before returning home.

Johnny and Bess stayed in Lille for almost five years, where Johnny's down-to-earth management style endeared him to his employees and employer. He was conscientious about his job and built his reputation on trust and dedication. His philosophy was that he would never ask anyone to do a job that he was not prepared to do himself. In return, he demanded and received the loyalty and support of his colleagues and employees.

International Harvester was doing well, so officials decided to open a plant closer to Paris in order to manufacture thrasher machines for shipment to North Africa. Ris-Orangis was selected as the site, and Johnny became works manager there on October 1, 1951. "I thought about it long and hard before accepting the company's offer," he admitted 40 years later. "It was a new adventure and a tremendous challenge."

The Mileses found a rundown, older house, rented it, and began another round of renovations. "Bess kept a loving eye on the workmen, supplied them with coffee, and practised her French," Johnny says. "She learned many of their trade secrets on repairing walls, painting, and finishing floors."

For the next two years, Johnny and Bess enjoyed life in this new home, which was supplemented by frequent trips to Paris. There they took advantage of the theatre, the arts, and the fine restaurants, and Bess became a student of French cuisine. Their return to North America in February 1954 brought some regrets.

For one thing, Johnny would not be rejoining his father. News of his death in September 1953 reached Johnny by telegram, and he responded by cable, indicating how difficult it would be to attend the funeral at that time. His family expressed understanding and urged him to stay on the job, but in retrospect, Johnny regrets not having attended. "My father and I were good friends through most of the years we lived together, travelled together, laughed—and almost cried—together," Johnny says, adding that the two had probably drifted apart because of the distance between them. "He was a great influence on me. I was proud to have him for a father." Bess claims that "to hear Johnny talk about his dad, you would think he was a saint." To which Johnny replies, "Maybe not a saint, but a good man."

The life awaiting Bess and Johnny in Chicago would prove very different from the one they left behind in France. They continue to cherish the seven years they spent there and have stayed in touch with many of their European friends for 35 years.

From International Harvester's point of view, Johnny had paid his dues, and his appointment as manager of manufacturing at the Chicago plant was a major promotion. He provided hands-on supervision to the twine mills in New Orleans and had many opportunities to visit his former workplace in Hamilton. As an advisor to the operations in France, Germany, and Sweden, he was able to share the experience he had garnered in France. Because his new job was extremely demanding, Johnny registered in the executive program at the University of Chicago.

Except for reading the annual Boston Marathon results, Johnny did not take a particular interest in road racing. He did, however, keep himself in top shape by working out twice a week at a health club. Few people knew that the slightly balding 50-year-old executive was the same Johnny Miles whose name had been blazoned across Chicago newspapers in 1926.

People were reminded of Johnny's achievements when he was inducted into the Canadian Sports Hall of Fame in 1967. He had heard from a colleague that someone from the Canadian National Exhibition in Toronto—where the hall of fame is located—was making inquiries about him, so he was not totally surprised when he received official notification of his selection. "It was a great honor, not only for me, but for Nova Scotia, my home province. That I should now be in the same illustrious company as the great stars of hockey, football, track and field, and other Canadian sports was a bit mind-boggling," says the ninth Nova Scotian chosen for the distinction. "I felt proud to be a Canadian, despite the fact that I was working at the time in the United States."

After Johnny received his Masters of Business Administration equivalency certificate, he was given a special assignment. With the advent of the European Common Market, he was delegated the task in 1965 of working with a team of consultants to study changing European business trends. Johnny visited all of the Common Market countries, and the group's final recommendations resulted in the construction of a state-of-the-art plant in northern France. He also visited Cuba on business only a few months before a young Fidel Castro led the overthrow of the government.

Johnny was transferred in 1968 to the farm-equipment division, as assistant manager of manufacturing. At about this time, the company was undergoing a major reorganization, and 62-year-old Johnny was offered early retirement. Satisfied with his 43-year corporate track record, he accepted the offer.

He had witnessed Harvester's heyday. In 1929, when Johnny had decided to devote his future to the company, Harvester's farm-equipment sales in North America were triple those of its nearest competitor, Deere and Company. With U.S. sales of $262 million, common stock peaked at $142 a share. By 1966, profits reached $109 million. But a period of decline followed, and between 1980 and 1984, accumulated loss for International Harvester reached nearly $3 billion. On November 26, 1984, officials announced that they were selling off most of the firm's farm-equipment assets in North America and Europe and were dropping the corporate name.

In Hamilton, the plant so familiar to Johnny no longer bore the International Harvester sign.

Johnny and Bess remained in Chicago in their East View Park home until early in 1971. He had been away for almost 25 years, but Johnny had no doubts that he wanted to retire in Canada.

12 The Johnny Miles Marathon

The Mileses decided to settle in Hamilton and chose a comfortable highrise apartment on Hamilton Mountain. They soon fell into a pleasant routine. Both in good health, Johnny and Bess developed a daily fitness regime and found new interests such as golfing, jogging, hiking, and cross-country skiing. They re-established family contacts, Johnny rejoined the Hamilton Olympic Athletic Club, and he was looking forward to attending the 1976 Olympics in Montreal.

He was not expecting anything out of the ordinary in late December 1974 when he opened his annual Christmas card from Dr. John Miles Williston, a Nova Scotia physician whom the Mileses had met in October 1956. He looked for the short note that was usually tucked inside but found instead a long letter proposing a 1975 marathon for New Glasgow, Nova Scotia, bearing Johnny's name.

Johnny did not know that Williston had attended a medical convention in Winnipeg, Manitoba, a few months before. Winnipeg was celebrating its centenary, and Williston, an active community volunteer and president of New Glasgow's recreation committee, was presented with a civic award. He returned to Nova Scotia brimming with ideas for the 1975 centennial celebrations in his home town, including a marathon.

New Glasgow—in Pictou County, on the northeast shore of Nova Scotia—had given Johnny one of his warmest receptions during the triumphant 1926 journey home from Boston. From the balcony of the Vendome Hotel, across the street from the train station, the mayor had introduced the young runner to the hundreds of people gathered below.

The New Glasgow Amateur Athletic Association presented a silver cup to Johnny, who had raced there on numerous occasions. It was reported that the crowd was one of the biggest to assemble in town since the end of World War I.

It was therefore no coincidence that Johnny's name popped up when the town's recreation committee sat down to plan a centennial marathon. One of the prime movers behind the proposal was Williston, known throughout the county as a "doer" who would not take no for an answer. He also knew Johnny.

The legendary runner had met the small-town doctor during a 1956 visit to Cape Breton. The Mileses were in Sydney Mines so Bess could experience the beauty of the landscape and warmth of the people of which Johnny had spoken so often. While in town, Johnny was interviewed on television by a local sportscaster, and Sydney native Malcolm Williston happened to be watching. He called to his brother, who was dining there that evening, and the doctor telephoned the television station asking that Johnny wait for him at the studio.

Within minutes, an emotional Williston was shaking the hand and slapping the back of a very surprised Johnny. Over coffee, Johnny learned that Williston had been named after him shortly after Williston's birth on May 23, 1927. Asked if she had decided on a name for her infant son, Williston's mother replied that she had a few ideas but was waiting to see if Johnny Miles won the 15-mile race in Glace Bay the next day. If so, she would name the baby John Miles Williston.

The two men could not spend much time together that evening, but they kept in touch thereafter.

"Name the centennial marathon after Johnny Miles," Williston told the town recreation committee, "and I'll guarantee that Miles will come to New Glasgow for the race." The chairman even promised that Johnny would donate a trophy for the event.

When Johnny read of the proposal, he told Bess immediately that, of course, he would lend his name to the marathon. He wrote Williston in early January and considered donating one of his prized trophies for the occasion, but he and Bess decided that a new marathon deserved a new trophy.

Williston and his committee set about receiving official sanction from the Nova Scotia Track and Field Association. Approval was far from automatic, however, and the committee grew worried: Without the association's seal of approval, many of the best long-distance runners would not attend. The track and field association expressed concern that a New Glasgow race would jeopardize participation in an existing marathon run each May in Yarmouth. But three months later, aware of the wide support that the New Glasgow contingent had mustered, the officials relented. The inaugural running of the Johnny Miles Marathon was slated for May 19, 1975.

From out of the archives, the organizing committee resurrected a photograph of Johnny crossing the Boston finish line in 1926. The photo was widely distributed and appeared on pins, in advertisements, and on posters. Replicas of the shirt he wore in 1926 were manufactured for distribution to all race participants.

Chosen as chief judge for the race was John "Brother" MacDonald, a well-known local broadcaster; honorary judge was Roland Sherwood, a former member of the Amherst (Nova Scotia) Athletic Club who had competed in many foot races throughout the Maritimes, including the 1925 Halifax marathon that was Johnny's stepping-stone to Boston. In addition to George Manos, timers were popular Pictou County runners of days gone by, Roy Oliver and Jimmie Hawboldt.

The event was shaping up into more than a foot race: A cultural program was planned with pipe bands, Highland dancers, a gymnastics display, and the singing of New Glasgow's own centennial song. Many old traditions were revived for the occasion.

Greetings were received from a wide range of people, including New Glasgow mayor M.A. Harquail, Nova Scotia education minister A. Garnet Brown, and Manitoba premier Edward Schreyer, a future governor general and honorary patron of the Johnny Miles Marathon.

The sun shone on race day as thousands of people turned out to witness the inaugural event. Near the finish line, spectators were packed 10 and 12 deep to watch the 27 entrants complete the course. Listed among the entrants, but not a finisher, was Number 14, Johnny Miles.

The first to finish was Chuck Davenport, a 41-year-old electrician from Eastern Passage, near Dartmouth, Nova Scotia. As soon as he broke the tape in 3:05.52, he collapsed into the arms of race chairman George MacKay and was placed immediately in a waiting ambulance. Davenport was examined and given oxygen, and not long after that, he received the trophy from a beaming Johnny.

The trophy was inscribed, "WINNER'S CHALLENGE TROPHY Donated by Johnny Miles, winner of the Boston Marathon, 1926, 29. In memory of Catherine Williston, who by naming a son after Johnny Miles set in

motion the events which ultimately led to the Johnny Miles Marathon."
Johnny had had the trophy engraved but had misspelled Mrs. Williston's
name, which is spelled with a "K."

Approximately five minutes behind Davenport was Frank Gervais, of
Halifax, and the third-place finisher was Neil Patrick MacMullin, a
student from Sydney Mines.

Pleased with the success of the centennial road race and overwhelmed
by the media interest in the event, the New Glasgow Recreation Committee lost no time in pondering the marathon's future. The committee was
well aware of the views of those who felt that Hawboldt and Oliver, who
were inducted with Johnny into the Nova Scotia Sports Heritage Hall of
Fame in 1980, should be given high priority when a permanent name was
chosen for the race.

The committee decided finally that the race should continue as a full
marathon and bear the name of Nova Scotia's most famous marathoner,
who had established world records while living in the province. Williston
and the committee went back to the track and field association to receive
sanction for an annual marathon. The request was granted in a matter of
months.

The race, held every Mother's Day, has become a celebration and is
recognized throughout North America for its challenging course, innova-
tive and imaginative organization, and smooth-running volunteer net-
work. Manos, for many years the general chairman of the marathon,
doubles as the voice atop the trailer who announces the name of each
runner crossing the finish line. Members of Williston's family are among
the most active race boosters. Daughter Beth and son Roy participated in
the early years of the run and, if they are in New Glasgow on race day, can
be assured of one task or another. Williston's sister Lorraine also helps out.
Although Williston's wife, Phyllis, carries no official title, her behind-the-
scenes contribution is invaluable. In 1985, Dr. Williston was the guest of
honor at the pre-race dinner and received a special gift—a striking painting
that intertwines the images of Williston and Johnny.

Well over 1,000 runners have entered "the Miles" since its inception,
and as it has grown, new events have been added. The half-marathon and
the mini-marathon, for young runners, are now producing a level of
competition comparable in many ways to that of the full marathon. Three
women—Beth Williston and Dawn Bryan, of New Glasgow, and Nancy
Plummer, of Baie Comeau, Quebec—finished the full marathon in 1976,
the first women to do so in Nova Scotia. Four years later, the Bess Miles

Trophy was first awarded to the top woman finisher. The Miles Marathon Committee has hosted the National Marathon Championships, in September 1978, and twice hosted the Masters Marathon Championship.

On several occasions, the race route has been altered because of a desire to find the right mixture of challenge, safety, efficiency, and spectator accessibility. Critics suggest that such changes makes it difficult to compare winners, but others say that varying climatic conditions, improvements in training and equipment, and a renewed awareness about fitness allow each winner to stand on his or her own record.

Bob Russell, of Dartmouth, has won the marathon eight times, earning him the nicknames "hot rod" and "King of the Johnny Miles Marathon." The race committee is considering giving him a replica of the trophy.

Among the spin-offs of any successful marathon is the impetus it provides for similar events in other communities. An example of this is the work of Sydney Mines fisherman Neil MacMullin, the third-place finisher in the inaugural run. MacMullin helps organize the annual Bill Taylor 10-mile Marathon and the Con Olson 15-mile event.

A popular feature of the New Glasgow marathon is the banquet, traditionally held on the eve of the race. Each year, one or more well-known people from the world of athletics is invited to speak. In 1976, Bruce Kidd, the outspoken Canadian three-miler who was named Canadian Press athlete of the year in 1962 and 1963, was the first of a long list of personalities to associate themselves with the Miles marathon. Banquet audiences have also been treated to tales from, among others, Abby Hoffman, Canada's 800-metre track hopeful at the 1972 Olympics, and Nancy Garapick, the Nova Scotia swimmer who won two bronze medals at the 1976 Olympics.

After Bill Rodgers won his third Boston Marathon in 1979, Williston had the opportunity to meet him and used the occasion to bend his ear about visiting New Glasgow. It would take him more than nine years to hook Rodgers, after three visits to Boston, volumes of correspondence, numerous telephone calls and, finally, an offer to cover Rodgers' expenses. The runner who had meanwhile won his fourth and final Boston Marathon said that he would attend in 1988.

Accompanied by his wife, Gail, Rodgers responded to the warm reception they received by joining in all of the weekend activities. He participated in a very successful panel on health and fitness and was at the starting line that Sunday to run the Johnny Miles Half-Marathon.

Wearing number 14—the number Johnny wore in Boston in 1926—Rodgers came in fifth. The man who had run his first Boston 21 minutes faster than Johnny ever had said he had not recovered well that year from Boston but had no complaints about the "shifting-your-gears type of course."

In 1979, the 50th anniversary of Johnny's second record-breaking performance in Boston, the guest speaker was from that city. Will Cloney, director of the Boston Athletic Association from 1946 to 1982, had been asked four years earlier by a reporter—before he had met Johnny—to predict the winner of that year's marathon and to choose the best Boston Marathon ever run. "Each race has a personality and a story of its own," Cloney responded. "They are all great ... but any marathon expert can give you a list of 20 names, and you can be sure the first ten runners will be on that list." He concluded the interview by adding, "There hasn't been a Johnny Miles since Johnny Miles."

In New Glasgow, Cloney entertained the audience with insiders' tidbits on planning the world-famous marathon. Organizers must arrange for 85 buses to take runners to the starting line, have 40,000 safety pins available to fasten numbers onto jerseys, and supply toilets along the route.

Recalling the 1926 running of the Boston Marathon, Cloney called Johnny's victory "sensational.... Miles was the first and last real surprise winner of the Boston Marathon."

Cloney—a former sportswriter, university professor, and investment counsellor—came back to New Glasgow in 1986 and spoke about the changes taking place within the Boston organization. The year before, it had been announced that "the Boston" would end 88 years of pure amateurism in 1986 and begin offering cash prizes. A new race sponsor, John Hancock Financial Services, would pay the winner $30,000, plus $25,000 if a course record were set and another $50,000 if a world record were set. For several years, the winner also received a Mercedes-Benz, but Mercedes has withdrawn its sponsorship. Another $145,000 was to be split among other categories.

Cloney supported the idea of awarding prizes in order to improve the image of the race—several of the major marathons around the world offer cash and prizes—but material gain had obviously had little to do with participation: From a group of 27 runners in 1897, the marathon had grown to accommodate thousands each year. "All the major races were paying money under the table. I absolutely refused," Cloney said in New Glasgow. "I'm not being critical of John Hancock ... but we didn't pay prize or appearance money the year Alberto Salazar won the Boston by two seconds [1982]. I think it has gone too far to the other extreme. My principle concern is that the BAA is lost in the shuffle."

Johnny responded to the news by saying, "I never made one cent in all my road-racing career."

Each year in New Glasgow, Johnny carries a heavy load as race patron, official starter, and host. He also participates in the annual workshops and, on numerous occasions, has given fitness seminars in local schools. He is a popular spokesman, and the media never tire of the recollections of his running days.

Johnny at Croix Twine Mill, France, 1948.

Bess and Johnny return to France from 1950 visit to Canada.

Poses for International Harvester Today *in Chicago, 1967.*

The Johnny Miles Marathon.

Bill Rodgers wins the 1979 Boston Marathon.

Johnny and John Williston at the annual New Glasgow marathon.

Lights the flame at the 1979 Canada-U.S. Games at
McMaster University, Hamilton.

13 Accolades and Honors

Strangely, Johnny did not return to Boston for 48 years. But as the 50th anniversary of his 1929 victory approached, he began to reflect on the idea of returning to the city and watching the race that had made him a star. With a bit of urging from Williston and an invitation from Will Cloney, Johnny and Bess agreed to accompany members of the Miles Marathon Committee to Boston for the 83rd running of the classic.

True to their expectations, there was a lot to watch, as 8,000 qualifiers and 3,000 others ran the course. They came from 50 U.S. states and 28 other countries, and 3,500 of them crossed the finish line in less that three hours. Among them was 71-year-old Johnny A. Kelley, who completed the 26 miles and 385 yards for the 48th time.

When Number 109 crossed the finish line, a cheer went up from the New Glasgow contingent: It was Fergie McKay, of Pictou County, Nova Scotia, finishing well out of the money but enjoying the fun of running in Boston for a third time. McKay is now a member of the Miles Marathon Committee.

Number one on the race program was William L. Rodgers, of Melrose. Less than two hours and 10 minutes after the start of the race, finish-line announcer Tom Grik shouted into his microphone, "Ladies and gentlemen, let's hear it. The greatest long-distance runner in the history of the world and the greatest runner alive today, ladies and gentlemen, Bill Rodgers."

As the crowd roared, "Rodgers, Rodgers, Rodgers," Johnny's thoughts drifted back to that day 50 years earlier when his name had been shouted to the heavens as he bowed his head to receive his second laurel wreath. From the stands in 1979, his eyes scanned the contestants looking for the familiar face of the late Clarence DeMar. Of all the runners with whom Johnny had shared the starting line, the sweaty locker rooms, and the muddy tracks and knee-shaking asphalt, DeMar "outclassed them all." Like Jimmie Henigan, Karl Koski, Silas McLellan, Whitey Michelson, and scores of others, DeMar was much older than Johnny, but they all shared things in common. They all ran for the joy of it, often belying their public images. Who would have guessed that the smile on Johnny's face as Rodgers crossed the finish line was not for "Boston Billy" but for DeMar? "I was thinking about the time an old friend chastised him for spending so much of his energy and time running those long-distance races for medals and silver cups. Clarence responded by asking, 'Do I owe you anything? If not, well, mind your own business, and I will mind mine,'" Johnny says. "On another occasion, a would-be friend stepped in front of DeMar during a race to offer an orange or a sponge. Without hesitation, though he apologized afterwards, he gave the intruder a straight-arm, sending the would-be benefactor flying."

It was a significant third Boston victory for Rodgers, and Johnny had no intention of upstaging the winner. But Johnny received more than his share of media attention, attending a press conference that received generous coverage. He also met Kelley, though he could not remember having run against him.

The real highlight of the Boston visit, however, was when Johnny received the Will Cloney Award in recognition of the golden anniversary of his 1929 victory and his contribution to the history of the marathon. Also present were Robert J. Scales, senior vice president of the Prudential Insurance Company—the major race sponsor—and Nova Scotia premier John Buchanan, who presented Johnny with a replica of the famous schooner *Bluenose*.

Johnny was introduced in 1979 to thousands of North Americans who had probably never heard his name. One month before the Boston visit, he had received the Dalhousie Award for Great Contribution to Nova Scotia Sports, at Dalhousie University in Halifax. Johnny was only the fourth recipient of the award, previously given to Henry Pelham, a rower from Herring Cove who won the prestigious Henley regatta in the early 1930s; Aileen Meagher, a former world-record holder in the 60-yard dash, from Halifax; and Sam Balcom, a great snow-shoe racer, also a Haligonian. "This year's deserving recipient ... was none other than John C. Miles, better known in provincial sports circles as Johnny," said the student newspaper, the *Dalhousie Gazette*. "At 73 years of age, this modest athlete has certainly fulfilled his life long belief that desire, skill and determination are the key to successful endeavors."

All of this was but a prelude to an official recognition from Canada. In 1980, one of Johnny's supporters wrote to Gerald Regan, a Nova Scotian then serving as federal sports minister, proposing that a postage stamp be struck in recognition of Johnny's double Boston win. Regan replied that various criteria surrounded the release of a stamp, including the fact that they are used to honor deceased people, but he suggested that Johnny be nominated for the Order of Canada, the nation's most prestigious award. Approximately 60 Canadians are so honored each year for achievements or for contributions to their community.

The application was sent in May 1981, along with the appropriate endorsements. Ontario premier William Davis said he had "no doubt that Mr. Miles would carry with dignity and responsibility any honor bestowed on him by his country." "I was impressed by him personally, as I am by his record as a sports figure and businessman over many years," wrote Nova Scotia premier John Buchanan. "Too often sportsmen forget or deflate the efforts and performances of previous generations ... but Miles, better than anyone else I know, communicates a vivid sense of the tradition of distance running in Canada," said Bruce Kidd, also a University of Toronto physical education professor. Nova Scotia senator Henry O. Hicks added that he had been a schoolboy when Johnny won in Boston, "and he was certainly the schoolboy's hero in Nova Scotia."

Johnny learned of the events when he received a letter from Ottawa in November 1982 asking if he would accept the award, providing the governor general approved the nomination. He agreed—and so did the governor general—and Johnny's name appeared on the list of recipients released that December. The process had been an extraordinarily fast one for someone not receiving the award based on a recent event.

He later told the *New Glasgow Evening News* that he "never expected such an honour" in his lifetime. "It's not going to change my life—same hat size and shirt size," he said.

Johnny, Bess, and some friends and family arrived in Ottawa the following spring for the April 20 ceremonies. The 77-year-old guest of honor was swamped with requests for interviews, including a live interview with popular CBC Radio host Peter Gzowski. There was also an afternoon reception for the Miles contingent, hosted by Governor General Edward Schreyer. In thanking the marathon committee for a scroll naming him honorary race patron, Schreyer recounted the story of how he first heard the name Johnny Miles. "It was during my university days and I was spending a summer at the military camp in Debert, Nova Scotia," he said. "The P.T. [physical training] instructor chided me for my seeming inexperience in track and field with the remark, 'You'll never be a Johnny Miles.'" Not knowing who this Miles was, Schreyer asked a fellow Royal Canadian Officers Training Corps student. The student told him, and Schreyer never forgot the name.

That evening in Rideau Hall, a nervous Johnny stood in a black tuxedo as Schreyer pinned on the badge of the Order of Canada—a cross of six arms enamelled white and representing a snow flake, centred by a maple leaf, surrounded by a red enamelled ring, surmounted by the royal crown, and inscribed with the motto of the order, DESIDERANTES MELIOREM PATRIAM (They Desire a Better Country). From now on, Johnny could add the initials "CM" after his name, standing for Canada Member.

The initials could have signified "child miner." He had indeed come a long way from the dingy, damp coal mine in Cape Breton where he had worked as a boy.

The list of recipients that evening read like a Canadian Who's Who, including author Morley Callaghan, Allan Gotleib, Canada's ambassador to the United States, popular singer and songwriter Bruce Cockburn, Diane Lynn Dupuy, founder and producer of the Famous People's Players, world-renowned skier Steve Podborski, and Nova Scotia's Eileen Cameron Henry, outstanding community volunteer.

"It's quite an honor," Johnny said during the festivities. "Canada is a wonderful country; it's my home. I feel proud and humble."

Following the formal evening ceremonies, there were several other receptions. In an Ottawa *Citizen* article headlined, "MARATHONER MILES, LEGITIMATE CANADIAN HERO," Johnny was quoted as saying, "From the bowels of the earth to this."

Johnny is inducted into the Canadian Sports Hall of Fame, 1967.

Visits Sam Keeling, 1983.

Receives the Order of Canada, 1983, from Governor General Ed Schreyer.

14 Remembered at Home

To travel with Johnny through the towns of Nova Scotia is somewhat akin to watching a long-lost son return home.

When the *Boston Post*'s Bill Cunningham and a photographer accompanied Johnny back to Cape Breton in 1926, they were amazed by the reception that met them at every whistle stop from Yarmouth to Sydney. Johnny was big news. More than 60 years later, middle-aged people as well as senior citizens remember his name, his exciting races, and his victories.

In a craft shop in St. Anns—a small community on Cape Breton's famous Cabot Trail—a woman overhears someone say that Johnny Miles is in the store. Isobel Crosby McAulay, from Nova Scotia's South Shore, introduces herself and recounts how, as a youngster, she watched Johnny race against Jimmie Henigan in Yarmouth. Later that autumn day in 1983, just down the road, Alec McLeod welcomes Johnny into his home. They have never met. McLeod recalls how he and his family were glued to the radio back in 1926 listening to a broadcast of the Boston Marathon. When asked what he remembers about the race, McLeod says, "I only remember that Jack won, and that was good enough for me." That afternoon in a popular Baddeck restaurant, Johnny is approached by several people, and he speaks with owner Tennyson MacDonald. Johnny has not seen MacDonald since 1927, when he and his brother Tom worked with MacDonald at the British Canadian Co-operative Store in Sydney Mines.

As we drive through Sydney Mines and North Sydney, Johnny's eyes light up. He retraces the route to "the Cranberry" district, where he ran along the snowy streetcar tracks, picks out the white house where his Uncle

Oscar once lived, and points to the Fahey Street Presbyterian Church his family attended. There is a new post office, but the co-operative store is still open and it still looks the same. The co-op has since closed.

We drive down Crescent and Cable streets, past the old Princess Mine wash plant, looking for the Miners' Museum. Johnny gets out of the car and asks a man for directions. When he mentions his name, the man looks at him in disbelief. "My God, it *is* Johnny Miles!" he exclaims. "Sure, I remember you. I even saw you run here, though I was only a wee b'y. You'll never be forgot down here." The man tells us that the museum is closed but takes us into a corner store run by Neil MacMullin, third-place finisher in the first Johnny Miles Marathon.

Johnny insists on visiting the Shore Road home his family occupied on Greener's Point. Another family is living there now, but he says that will not be a problem. And it is not. The Caldwells invite us in and treat Johnny as if he were their son. "Let us know the next time you plan to come this way," Mrs. Caldwell says. "We'd like to have you speak to our historical society."

Passing Little Pond, on the way to Florence, Johnny sees a sign marked "LeBlanc Road." "Turn down here," he says excitedly. "I think Sam Keeling lives somewhere close by." We ask who Keeling is, and he explains that Keeling is the one who first suggested that Johnny take up running, passing along the Alfred Shrubb book as well. "He gave it to me in 1922, and I guess I haven't seen Sam since 1927." He points out a house, and we drive into a big yard and up to a house with a large letter "K" on the front door. "Are you sure this is it? What if Sam has passed away?" someone asks doubtfully. But Johnny is taking the steps two at a time and knocking on the door.

There is a pause, and we are just about to leave when a wizened old man opens the door and looks up. Before he can say anything, Johnny laughs excitedly and says, "How's it going, Sam? Boy, oh boy, is it good to see you." Keeling's eyes light up as he recognizes the voice from the past. "Oh my God! Jack, Jack Miles!" Not waiting for a response and not inviting us in out of the wind, Keeling continues. "This is the first time you've come to see me since you've come down here." Johnny apologizes for not having made more of an effort to see Keeling on other occasions, and Keeling moves on to questions about Johnny's family. "I always liked Lena," he says.

The wind seems to have died down, and we sit on the porch as Keeling and Johnny reminisce. Keeling recalls the wonderful reception Johnny received on his 1926 homecoming and the last time he saw Johnny run, 1930, in Boston. "Don't do much running now," says the 84-year-old Keeling, who has since passed away. "Still play tennis on my court there."

Keeling is beginning to tire, but he invites us inside to rout through a box of old newspaper clippings and faded photographs. "Here, Jack, take these pictures. I've been saving them for you, hoping that some day we would meet again." The photos are all from the September 5, 1925, national track and field championship held in Halifax. As we are leaving the house, we encounter his daughter Edna, who tells Johnny that her father speaks frequently of his old friend Jack.

Passing through Florence, Johnny shows us where he attended school on Main Street, points out the former site of the No. 4 mine and the Green Hill house where he spent his early youth. "I'll never forget Taffy Williams, an old Welshman who lived opposite the Florence co-operative store. He used to make spruce beer. Even though my father never drank the stuff, he would send me to pick some up to give to the men who were building this house. They liked it, especially on hot days."

Johnny's usual reticence seems to have disappeared as we drop into several other residences—warmly welcomed in every one. All of this confirms what we already know: Even such a long time after Johnny moved to Ontario, his name and his feats are still alive and well in the hearts of Nova Scotians.

Each time he returns to Hamilton from a visit to Nova Scotia, he reflects on the day, more than 60 years before, when he crossed the Strait of Canso to take up residence in Ontario. "I remember that we had a feeling of brotherhood in our community, and I will never forget it," he says. "I am sure that even today, as young people on the island go through their struggle to go or stay, they have a similar gnawing inside them, wondering if, indeed, they do go, will they ever be able to come back home again. For me, it took a long time to make it back to my home town, and I appreciate everything that the people of the island have given to me."

In 1989, Sydney Mines celebrated its 100th birthday, and Johnny was invited to attend. During his visit, he had the opportunity to meet many old friends, and he was particularly pleased to speak with Sam Selfridge, one of the boys with whom he had worked in the coal mine during World War I. He also used the occasion to return the Nate Nathansan cup to Nathansan's son Norris in hopes that the race will be revived.

One of the official events was the Johnny Miles Homecoming, held on Saturday, July 22, and including a public reception and the running of the Johnny Miles Centennial Three-Mile Race. Donnie Sexton, of Stellarton, Nova Scotia, won over a field of 65 entries, in a time of 17:50. Later, Johnny toured a new Sydney Mines sports complex—the Johnny Miles Gymnasium.

Johnny is still a role model for aspiring young athletes. As a director of the Hamilton Olympic Athletic Club, he maintains a close contact with the athletes and is a strong supporter of the Olympic movement. He says he is worried by the advent of "advertisement-oriented athletes. In my day, the ultimate goal was to be selected as a member of your national Olympic team and represent your country in competition against the best amateur athletes in the world, for the love of the Games. Today, sports are more commercialized."

The oldest living winner of the Boston Marathon, who marked his 84th birthday on October 30, 1989, is still working for the cause of clean sports.

Appendix

Chronological Listing, Johnny Miles' Major Races

Place	Distance	Date	Position	Selected Times
1922				
Sydney	3-mile/road	May 24	17th	
North Sydney	3-mile/road	July 1	3rd	
Sydney Mines	3-mile/road	Aug. 1	4th	
1923				
Sydney/Whitney Pier	3-mile/road	May 24	2nd	
North Sydney	3-mile/road	July 2	1st	
Antigonish Highland Games	5-mile/road	Aug. 23	2nd	
Sydney Mines	3-mile/road	Sept. 3	1st	
Halifax (Canadian championship)	5-mile/track	Sept. 15		
1924				
Sydney/Whitney Pier	3-mile/road	May 24	2nd	
1925				
Sydney/Whitney Pier	3-mile/road	May 25	1st	15:18
Sydney	1-mile/track	July 1	1st	
Dartmouth	6-mile/road	Aug. 6	1st	31:20
Baddeck	1-mile/road	Aug. 21	2nd	
Halifax (Canadian championship)	5-mile/track	Sept. 5	1st	26:50
Halifax (Canadian championship)	1 mile	Sept. 5	3rd	
Amherst	10-mile/track	Sept. 7	1st	53:48.05
Antigonish	5-mile/track	Oct. 15	1st	
Halifax	10-mile/road	Oct. 17	1st	53:48.6
1926				
Boston	26 mi, 209 yd	April 19	1st	2:25.40.4
Sydney	3-mile/road	May 24	1st	15:18
North Sydney	6-mile/indoor (against relay team)	May 3	1st	38:09
Stellarton	5-mile/track	June 2	1st	27:46
Amherst	10-mile/track	June 3	1st	56:26
Melrose, Mass.	10-mile/track	June 12	did not finish	

Halifax	10-mile/track	July 1	1st	54:14.2
Margaree Forks	5-mile/track	July 16	1st	
Antigonish	5-mile/track	July 21	2nd	
Yarmouth	10-mile/track	July 23	1st	58:22.05
Boston (Caledonia Games)	15-mile/track	August 7	1st	1:33.12.4
Sydney	10-mile/track	Aug. 13	4th	
Kentville	5-mile/track	Aug. 18	1st	26:5
Pictou	5 mile/track	Sept. 1	1st	26:57
Moncton, N.B.	5-mile/track	Sept. 6	1st	27:11.8
New Glasgow	5-mile/track	Sept. 8	1st	
Westville	5-mile/track	Sept. 11	2nd	
Charlottetown, P.E.I.	5-mile/track	Sept. 24	1st	27:43.2
Sydney	10-mile/track	Oct. 6	1st	57:19.2
Halifax	10-mile/road	Oct. 23	2nd	54:53.6
1927				
Boston	26 mi, 385 yd	April 19	did not finish	
Glace Bay	5 miles	May 24	1st	1:25.7.05
Buffalo, N.Y.	26 mi, 385 yd	May 30	3rd	
Halifax	10 miles	June 21	1st	53:32.4
Hamilton, Ont.	26 mi, 385 yd	Sept. 15	9th	3:23.28
Halifax	26 mi, 385 yd	Nov. 7	1st	2:40.29.2
1928				
Toronto	15-mile/road	April 13	did not finish	
Toronto	10,000-m/track	June 23	1st	33:46.4
Hamilton	10,000-m/track	July 2	1st	33:49.4
Amsterdam (Olympics)	26 mi, 385 yd	August 5	16th	2:43.32
1929				
Toronto	15-mile/road	March 29	1st	1:23.50
Boston	26 mi, 385 yd	April 20	1st	2:33.8.8
Glace Bay	10-mile/track	June 11	5th	
Hamilton	26 mi, 385 yd	Sept. 21	1st	2:46.25
1930				
Boston	26 mi, 385 yd	April 19	11th	2:55.08.4
Sydney Mines	10-mile/road	July 1	3rd	
Hamilton (British Empire Games)	26 mi, 385 yd	Aug. 21	3rd	2:40.30
1931				
Toronto	15-mile/road	March 27	5th	
Boston	26 mi, 385 yd	April 19	10th	3:4.56
London, Ont.	26 mi, 385 yd	May 26	3rd	2:47.12
Hamilton	26 mi, 385 yd	Sept. 19	2nd	
1932				
Los Angeles (Olympics)	26 mi, 385 yd	August 7	14th	2:50.32

Johnny Miles' Titles and Awards

Nova Scotia 10-mile record, 1925
Canadian 5-mile champion, 1925
Maritime 10-mile champion, 1926
Boston Marathon record and world marathon record, 1926
Canadian 10,000-metre record, 1928
Ontario 10,000-metre record, 1928
Boston Marathon record and U.S. National Marathon Championship, 1929
Marathon bronze medalist, first British Empire Games, 1930
Member, Canadian Sports Hall of Fame, 1967
Will Cloney Award, 1979
Dalhousie Award for Great Contribution to Nova Scotia Sports, 1979
Member, Nova Scotia Sports Heritage Hall of Fame, 1980
Member, Order of Canada, 1983

Canadian Winners, Boston Marathon

Year	Name/Age	Time	Occupation	Place of Birth
1898	R.J. MacDonald, 22	2:42	student	Antigonish, N.S.
1900	Jack Caffery, 20	2:29.23	laborer	Hamilton, Ont.
1901	Jack Caffery, 21	2:29.23	laborer	Hamilton, Ont.
1907	Tom Longboat, 19	2:24.24	farmer	Toronto, Ont.
1910	Fred Cameron, 23	2:28.52	printer	Amherst, N.S.
1914	James Duffy, 23	2:25.01	stonecutter	Hamilton, Ont.
1915	Edouard Fabre, 29	2:31.41	steel worker	Montreal, Que.
1926	John C. Miles, 20	2:25.40	delivery clerk	Sydney Mines, N.S.
1929	John C. Miles, 23	2:33.08	factory laborer	Hamilton, Ont.
1934	Dave Komonen, 35	2:32.53	mine worker	Sudbury, Ont.
1937	Walter Young, 24	2:33.20	unemployed	Verdun, Que.
1940	Gerard Cote, 26	2:28.28	news vendor	Valleyfield, Que.
1943	Gerard Cote, 29	2:28.25	soldier	Valleyfield, Que.
1944	Gerard Cote, 30	2:31.50	soldier	Valleyfield, Que.
1948	Gerard Cote, 34	2:31.02	hospital worker	St. Hyacinthe, Que.
1977	Jerome Drayton, 32	2:14.46	civil servant	Toronto, Ont.

Winners, Herald and Mail 10-Mile Modified Marathon

Year	Name	Time
1907	Hans Holmer, Halifax	59:29.8
1908	Hans Holmer, Halifax	57:57
1909	Fred Cameron, Amherst	56:52.2
1910	Michael Thomas, Charlottetown	58:52
1911	Michael Thomas, Charlottetown	58:41
1912	Michael Thomas, Charlottetown	58:30.2

1913 Victor MacAulay, Windsor   55:53.8
Suspended during World War I
1919 Alfred Rodgers, Halifax   57:44
1920 Alfred Rodgers, Halifax   62:06
1921 Victor MacAulay, Windsor   55:35.4
1922 Victor MacAulay, Windsor   54:29.4
1923 Victor MacAulay, Windsor   55:5
1924 Victor MacAulay, Windsor   57:08.6
1925 Johnny Miles, Sydney Mines   53:48.4
1926 Charles Snell, Toronto   54:14.8
1927 George Irwin, Dartmouth   54:23.8
1928 Ronald O'Toole, St. John's   53:00.8
1929 George Irwin, Dartmouth   54:36.4
1930 George Irwin, Dartmouth   54:27.4
1931 Roy Oliver, New Glasgow   54:20
1932 Roy Oliver, New Glasgow   53:45
1933 Noel Paul, Springhill Junction   53:27
1934 Roy Oliver, New Glasgow   51:50.2
1935 Johnny Kelley, Arlington, Mass.   51:32
1936 Con Olson, North Sydney   52:58
1937 Roy Oliver, New Glasgow   52:54
1938 Con Olson, North Sydney   56:08
1939 Leroy White, Amherst   56:18
Suspended during World War II
1944 Len Doiron, Aldershot   52:08
1945 John Paul, Charlottetown   52:46
Revived, the Halifax Herald Modified Marathon
1982 Greg Meyer, Grand Rapids, Mich. 50:50
      Jeannie Cameron, Halifax   62:54
1983 Ralph Williams, Centreville   51:37
      Jeannie Cameron   63:04
1984 Robert Englehutt, Dartmouth   51:12
      Bonnie LeFrank, Halifax   63:31
1985 Norm Tinkham, Halifax   50:10
      Bonnie LeFrank, Halifax   58:23
1986 Dan Kontak, Halifax   51:14
      Rebecca Richards, Middleton   60:58
1987 Dan Kontak, Halifax   51:46
      Bonnie LeFrank, Halifax   58:03
1988 Dan Kontak, Halifax   52:18
      Bonnie LeFrank, Halifax   59:47
1989 Bo MacGillivray   51:35
      Bonnie LeFrank, Halifax   1:01.17

Winners, Johnny Miles Marathon
First man and woman to finish*

Year	Name	Time
1975	Charles E. Davenport	3:05.52
1976	Harry Welles	2:39.08
	Beth Williston	4:08.06
1977	Pat Burke	2:38.21
	Dana Hovey	4:06.59
1978	Pat Burke	2:38.43
	Hilary Earp	4:02.28
1979	Dave Fudge	2:38.17.2
	Sarita Earp	3:47.42.8
1980	Dan Kontak	2:36.20.2
	Beverley Burchell	3:36.24
1981	Bob Russell	2:36.22
	Monica Lapointe	3:16.56
1982	Bob Russell	2:36.02
	Louise Brill	3:22.18
1983	Bob Russell	2:34.11
	Donna Osborne	3:49.63
1984	Bob Russell	2:32.56
	Beverley (Burchell) Williams	3:25.18
1985	Harold "Bo" MacGillivray	2:25.36
	Beverley Williams	3:28.39
1986	Bob Russell	2:29.45
	Beverley Williams	3:09.19
1987	Bob Russell	2:40.17
	Linda Ivany	4:00.37
1988	Bob Russell	2:33.34
	Holly Whitman	3:13.08
1989	Bob Russell	2:35.58
	Pam Power-McKenna	3:12.22

*Since 1980, the first woman to finish has been awarded the Bess Miles Trophy.

Winners, Challenge Trophy
Awarded to first man in masters category to complete full marathon

Year	Name	Time
1978	Wendall Kerr	2:53.42
1979	Ray Will	2:42.59
1980	Wendall Kerr	2:53.07
1981	Benjamin Johns	2:51.03

1982	Victor MacLeod	2:54.09
1983	Charlie Grant	2:55.18
1984	Walter Williams	2:42.58
1985	Walter Williams	2:44.31
1986	Joe McGuire	2:30.14
1987	Neil Ashton	3:03.29
1988	Jim Wyatt	2:48.15
1989	Walter Williams	2:48.40

Winners, The Half-Marathon
First man and woman to finish

Year	Name	Time
1981	Tom Olson	1:04.54
	Jeannie Cameron	1:19.31
1982	Freeman Churchill	1:06.57
	Jeannie Cameron	1:16.46
1983	Craig Parsons	1:13.36
	Jeannie Cameron	1:20.21
1984	Norm Tinkham	1:11.4
	Debbie Murphy	1:34.05
1985	Michael Hamilton	1:10.48
	Rebecca Richards	1:21.34
1986	Michael Hamilton	1:10.13
	Rebecca Richards	1:21.08
1987	Smartex Tambala	1:09.4
	Debbie Murray	1:30.51
1988	Paul McCloy	1:06.32
	Michele Granger	1:32.58
1989	Ron Jeppeson	1:14.5
	Beverley Williams	1:29.09

Sports Quiz

1. Who was the oldest person to win the Boston Marathon? Who is the oldest living winner of the Boston Marathon, as of 1989?
2. Who won the Herald and Mail 10-Mile Modified Marathon more often than any other? How many times, and in what year did he win the first time?
3. Who had the most second-place finishes in the Boston Marathon?
4. Name the runners who had back-to-back Olympic and Boston marathon wins.
5. Who was the only known Maritime runner to die as a direct result of participating in a long-distance race?.
6. Who caused the only false start at the Boston Marathon? What was his

nationality, and in what year did it happen?

7. Who was the heaviest winner of the Boston Marathon? What was his weight and the year he won?

8. What was the least number of entries in the Boston Marathon? In what year, and who was the winner?

9. Two of the greatest long-shot winners in Boston were Canadian. Who were they, and what did they have in common?

10. Only two American winners of the Boston won the Herald and Mail 10-Mile Modified Marathon in Halifax. Who were they, and in what years?

11. Which winner of the Boston came from the furthest back to win? Where was he born, and in what year did he win?

12. Who is the most-frequent winner of the Johnny Miles Marathon?

13. An aboriginal Canadian and an aboriginal American stand out as great competitors in the Boston Marathon. Who are they, and when did they win?

14. What and when was the greatest sweep by one nation, other than the U.S.A., in Boston? Who was the front runner?

15. Who was the first official women's winner? What was the name of the first Canadian woman to win?

16. Name the Canadian who won the most times in Boston. When?

17. Silas McLellan had three main loves. What were they?

18. Two incidents related to heart murmurs occurred at the Boston Marathon. Who were the runners who experienced them, and what impact did it have on their careers?

19. Who was Sam Keeling?

20. What were the four most-common occupations of Boston Marathon winners?

Answers:

1. Clarence DeMar, in 1930, a few days shy of his 42nd birthday. Johnny Miles, who turned 84 on October 30, 1989.

2. Victor MacAulay, of Windsor, N.S., won five times, the first time in 1913.

3. Johnny A. Kelley, Arlington, Mass., finished second on seven occasions: 1934, '37, '40, '41, '42, '44, '46. He finished first in 1935 and 1945.

4. None. No runner has ever won in Boston directly after winning an Olympic marathon.

5. Billy Taylor, of Sydney Mines, in Montreal on June 14, 1931.

6. John N. Barnard, Hamilton, Ont., dashed off before the signal in 1900, causing the only false start in the history of the BAA classic.

7. Cambridge, Mass., blacksmith Lawrence Brignolia weighed 173 pounds when he won in 1899. After stepping on a stone, he sat on the curb for three minutes before continuing and still won by three minutes.

8. In 1897, the first running of the race, 18 people registered, but only 15 showed at the starting line. John J. McDermot, of Pastime Athletic Club, New York, led the 10 finishers in 2:55.10.

9. Fred Cameron, of Amherst, N.S., was a 23-year-old apprentice-machinist

who had never run a marathon before his 1910 victory in Boston. He led from start to finish. Johnny Miles ran only one practice marathon before winning in Boston in 1926.

10. The elder John Kelley won in Boston and Halifax in 1935. Greg Meyer, of Wellesley, Mass., won in Boston and Halifax in 1982.

11. Henri Renaud—of Nassau, N.H., but thought to have been born in Trois-Rivières, Que.—was 53rd in Framington in 1909 before gaining the lead two miles from the finish to beat his closest competitor by four minutes.

12. Bob Russell, of Dartmouth, N.S., won in 1981, '82, '83, '84, '86, '87, '88, and '89.

13. Tom Longboat, a 19-year-old Onondago Indian from Six Nations Reserve near Brantford, Ont., won in Boston in 1907. He and eight others managed to avoid a freight train, leaving the rest of the runners on the other side of the tracks. Ellison M. "Tarzan" Brown, a 22-year-old Narragansett Indian from Alton, R.I., led from the start in 1936 and won again in 1939.

14. There have been several. In 1900, three Hamilton, Ont., runners—Jack Caffery, Bill Sherring, and Frank Hughson—finished first, second, and third. In 1950, Korean runners Kee Yong Ham, Kil Yoon Song, and Yun Chil Choi finished first, second, and third. In 1965, five Japanese runners took first, second, third, fifth, and sixth places, led by Morio Shigematsu. In 1966, Kenji Kimihara led four Japanese runners in nabbing first, second, third, and fourth places.

15. Nina Kuscik, a 33-year-old from South Huntington, N.Y., won in 1972. Montrealer Jacqueline Gareau, 27, won in 1980.

16. Gerard Cote, a 26-year-old from St. Hyacinthe, Que., won the first time in 1940 and again in 1943, '44, and '48. He is reported to have run more than 100,000 miles.

17. McLellan's three loves were ice cream, dancing, and running.

18. In 1911, Clarence DeMar was advised that he had a heart murmur but won the Boston Marathon that year. After the doctor died of a heart condition, DeMar suggested that the doctor must have been listening to his own heart. In 1958, three runners—Ted Corbitt, John Lafferty, and Al Confalone—were rejected from entering the Boston because the medical team detected heart murmurs in all three. Although they were not issued numbers, they ran and finished sixth, seventh, and ninth respectively, after giving the others a 100-yard head start.

19. Sam Keeling, of Sydney Mines, N.S., first introduced Johnny Miles to road racing and advised him to use the Alfred Shrubb training manual. Keeling was well known in Cape Breton as a 100-yard and 200-yard sprinter.

20. Clerk, student, teacher, and runner. Only one winner listed as being unemployed.

Extra:

The four most-popular first names of winners in the Boston Marathon to 1988 were: John, five times, James three times, Ron and Tom, twice each.

Selected
Bibliography

Bannister, Roger *First Four Minutes*. London: Putnam, 1955.

Bird, Will R. *This Is Nova Scotia*. Toronto: McGraw-Hill Ryerson, 1972.

Blaikie, David *Boston, The Canadian Story*. Ottawa: Seneca House Books, 1984.

Bloom, Marc *The Runner's Bible*. Garden City, N.Y.: Doubleday and Company, 1986.

Brown, Skip, and John Graham *Target 26*. Toronto: Collier MacMillan, 1979.

Commonwealth Games Association of Canada *Canada at the XII Commonwealth Games*. 1982.

Cumming, John *Runners and Walkers*. Chicago: Regnery Gateway, 1981.

DeMar, Clarence *Marathon*. Vermont: Stephen Daye Press, 1937.

Encyclopedia of Track and Field. New York: Prentice Hall, 1983.

Falls, Joe *The Boston Marathon*. New York: MacMillan, 1977.

Ferguson, Bob *Who's Who in Canadian Sport*. Toronto: Summerhill Press, 1985.

Fixx, James F. *The Complete Book of Running*. New York: Random House, 1977.

Foxborough, Henry *Great Days in Canadian Sports*. Toronto: Ryerson Press, 1957.

Friedberg, Ardy *How to Run Your First Marathon*. New York: Simon & Schuster, 1982.

Harris, Emerson P. *Co-operation: The Hope of the Consumer*. New York: Arno Press, 1976.

Henderson, Joe *The Complete Marathoner*. California: World/Mountain View, 1978.

Higdon, Hal *The Marathoners*. Toronto: Academic Press, 1980.

Hosker, Ray *Boston, America's Oldest Marathon*. California: Anderson World.

Howell, Maxwell L., and Reet A. Howell *History of Sports in Canada*. Champaign, Ill.: Stipes Publishing Co., 1981.

Howell, Nancy, and Maxwell Howell *Sports and Games in Canadian Life: 1700 to the Present*. Toronto: MacMillan of Canada, 1969.

Kidd, Bruce *Tom Longboat*. Toronto: Fitzhenry & Whiteside, 1980.

Kieran, John, Arthur Daley and Pat Jordan *The Story of the Olympic Games: 776 B.C. to 1964*. Philadelphia: Lippincott, 1965.

Larson, Etchello, Tulloh *The Marathon Book.* London: Virgin Books, 1982.

Lebow, Fred, and Richard Woodley *Inside the World of Big-Time Marathoning.* New York: Rawson Associates, 1984.

MacPherson, Ian *Each for All: A History of the Co-operative Movement in English Canada, 1900-1945.* Toronto: MacMillan of Canada, Carlton Library, 1979.

McEwan, Paul *Miners and Steelworkers.* Toronto: Stevens, Hakkert, 1976.

Mellor, John *The Company Store.* Halifax: Formac Publishing, 1983.

Neft, Johnson and Associates *All-Sports World Record Book.* New York: Grosset and Dunlap, 1976.

O'Donnell, John *The Men of the Deeps.* Waterloo, Ont.: Waterloo Music Co., 1975.

O'Toole, Ed *The Marathon Man: A Decade of Running.* St. John's, Nfld., 1982.

Redmond, Gerald *Caledonia Games: 19th Century America.* Cranberry, New Jersey, 1971.

Rodgers, Bill *Marathoning.* New York: Simon & Schuster, 1980.

Roxborough, Henry *Canada at the Olympics.* Toronto: Ryerson, 1963.

Schapp, Richard *An Illustrated History of the Olympics.* New York: Knopf, 1963.

Schrodt, B., G. Redmond and R. Baka *Sports Canadiana.* Edmonton, 1980.

Tewsley, Bob *Where to Run in Canada.* Ottawa: Deneau and Greenberg, 1980.

Treadwell, Sandy, *The World of Marathons.* New York: Stewart, Tabori and Chang, 1987.

Trout, Charles H. *Boston: The Great Depression and the New Deal.* New York: Oxford University Press, 1977.

Wallechinsky, David *The Complete Book of the Olympics.* London: Penguin, 1988.

Wise, S.F., and Douglas Fisher *Canada's Sporting Heroes.* Toronto: General Publishing, 1974.

Woods, Karl M. *The Sports Success Book.* Austin, Texas: Copperfield Press, 1985.

Young, Sandy *Beyond Heroes: A Sport History of Nova Scotia.* Hantsport: Lancelot Press, 1988.

Zeman, Brenda *To Run with Longboat.* Edmonton: GMS Ventures, 1988.